JOURNEY
TO THE
SUN

THE JOURNEY OF TEI FU CHEN
THE LEGACY OF SUNRIDER INTERNATIONAL

BY ROBERT A. HENRIE

Library of Congress Catalog Card Number: 99-073647

ISBN 0-9673432-0-8

First Printing, 1999

Printed in the United States of America

JOURNEY
TO THE
SUN

This chronicle of Tei Fu and Oi-Lin's journey has been dedicated to their children: Wendy, Reuben, Sunny, Eric, and Jonathan.

This book is dedicated as well to my own five children: Kinsi, Brittany, Brandon, Jordyn, and Wes.

The legacy of Sunrider International includes the journeys of thousands of people who have also dedicated their paths to the generations who will follow.

Good timber does not grow in ease.
The stronger winds, the tougher trees.
The further sky, the greater length,
The more the storm, the more the strength.
By sun and cold, by rain or snow,
In trees, or man, good timbers grow.

Where thickest stands the forest growth,
We find the Patriarchs of both;
Who hold a converse with the stars,
Whose broken branches show the scars
Of many winds and much of strife,
This is the common law of life.

———Author Unknown

CONTENTS

ACKNOWLEDGMENTS

With the support and encouragement of many people, this book was written. I appreciate everyone who extended a helping hand.

Dr. Oi-Lin Chen has been extremely diligent in seeing this project through to completion. She has a keen eye for detail and an unfailing memory. Her determination made this book possible.

Chris Knoles and Cathie DeNaughel cheerfully and competently assisted with many important production elements.

To Lee Roderick and Lisa Hartman, I must say— without you this book would never have been completed! Your commitment, your talent, and your sacrifices made mine much more bearable. Thank you for going the distance with me.

The Highway to Boron

The hour-and-twenty-minute Delta flight from Salt Lake City to Los Angeles was not much of a journey. Having flown to California once a week for nearly ten years, it was really more of a commute. Since 1989, I have been a marketing and communications consultant to Drs. Tei Fu and Oi-Lin Chen. Their company, Sunrider International, is a client of my advertising and marketing communications company. During the past decade I have worked closely with the Chens and Sunrider in developing their marketing/communications tools, including corporate literature and most of their promotional and training videos. Over that time, I have spent literally hundreds of hours with the Chens. I have come to know this Chinese couple in a very deep sense, both professionally and personally. Besides being clients, they have become my friends.

My acquaintance with the Chens began in 1983, when I moved from Washington, D.C. to Orem, Utah. After spending seven years in the Washington area working for a U.S. Congressman, I took a job in Utah as the corporate communications vice president for a large mining and transportation company. Our family, including my wife and children, moved into a pretty neighborhood in Orem, developed in a pear and apricot orchard. A few houses down the street lived a young Chinese couple who had a family of their own.

I had never formally met the Chens. One day, however,

my five-year-old daughter, Brittany, rode her tricycle down a flight of outdoor concrete steps which resulted in a small gash over her right eye. Rather than take her to the hospital emergency room, I called my neighbor, Oi-Lin Chen, who I knew was a medical doctor practicing out of a small office in the basement of her home.

Mrs. Chen sewed up the cut with three or four stitches. She was polite and professional. I asked about her family and her husband's occupation.

"Oh, he has just started a company that deals with Chinese herbs," she said simply. She did not elaborate.

Having never heard of Chinese herbs, I was curious, but I inquired no further. Six years would pass before we would meet again and my thoughts would return to Chinese herbs.

My flight arrived in Los Angeles in the early afternoon. I rented a car and began the two-and-a-half-hour drive from the airport across the high desert of Southern California to a remote, desolate mining community called Boron. It was there, at a federal detention facility, that I was scheduled to meet my friend and client, Dr. Tei Fu Chen.

Dr. Chen had already been incarcerated for about six weeks of a potential two-year sentence. A heavy spring rain was falling as I drove. It renewed the desert with a clean, refreshing smell of sagebrush; desert flowers blossomed everywhere. The drive was quiet, almost relaxing. Still, I felt a great sense of apprehension. I had never been inside a federal prison facility and had no idea what to expect. More compelling was my concern about how the incarceration had affected Tei Fu Chen. Of all the hardships and challenges he had faced in his dynamic life, surely this one must be the most difficult. This would be *the test*.

The Boron Federal Detention Camp was several miles outside of Boron, surrounded by nothing but desert. I felt some sense of relief as the facility came into sight. To my left was a baseball field. Straight ahead was a parking lot surrounded by fifteen to twenty cinder block buildings arranged in a campus style. It looked more like a complex of government buildings than a prison. There was no substantial fence, no barbed wire, no security towers or guards on patrol.

After parking, I walked into an administration office and filled out some simple paperwork. The guard was friendly and conversational. A heavy door opened that gave me access to a visiting room that resembled a cafeteria. Inside were roughly twenty tables surrounded by chairs. Since it was midweek and not regular visiting hours, only a few inmates were there, talking quietly with their families. I sat down at a table and waited for Dr. Chen to arrive.

Tei Fu Chen is easy to like. He's friendly, outgoing, and confident. He smiles often and easily and carries himself in such a commanding way that people notice him when he enters a room.

As he walked briskly into the visiting room, Tei Fu's broad smile gave me a sense of relief. Still, seeing him dressed in the prison-issue khaki pants and shirt, wearing work boots and carrying a dark denim coat, nearly took my breath away. It was almost like seeing someone in a hospital bed after an accident. You glimpse the reality of the trauma.

For some two hours we sat and talked. As always, we

ate while we talked. Both Tei Fu and I share a passion for eating. Through our years of association, he had taken me to some of the outstanding restaurants in the world. That day at Boron, we ate microwaved chicken wings and cantaloupe wrapped in cellophane that came from vending machines.

We talked of his daily schedule at the facility, and many other things, small and large. We discussed world issues, including the collapse of much of the Asian economy. And we talked of Sunrider and routine issues that faced the company and its distributors.

Then Chen spoke about the things that meant the very most to him—his wife and children, his religious beliefs, and his philosophies of herbs, of health, and of life. He was introspective, speaking little of the future; only of the core values and beliefs that would enable him to live through the days ahead.

I wanted to discuss the injustices and failures that had resulted in his incarceration. I was still angry with the American justice system, and with life's supposed rules of fairness. But he brushed it all off with "It's in the past."

One thing that Chen had not been able to reconcile or put behind him was his deep sorrow over the role his parents and two sisters had played in the previous ten years that resulted in a great deal of heartache and ultimately his sentence to Boron. His pain was unspeakable. The only way he could describe his hurt was to say, "I feel like the sharp fangs of a huge snake have pierced my heart." I couldn't discuss the subject further with him; emotions of the day were already running high.

The rain had ceased before my drive back to Los Angeles. The clouds were scattered and the sun settled into a brick-red western sky. I felt both a great relief and a sense of calm. The day had left a deep impression on me. It seemed to distill in my mind much of what I had witnessed during my ten-year involvement with Sunrider.

The story of Sunrider and Tei Fu and Oi-Lin Chen has been told in bits and pieces thousands of times by thousands of others. Never has their history been told in its entirety. Quite simply, Sunrider is one of the greatest entrepreneurial success stories of all time. It is the quintessential fulfillment of the American Dream—a story of extraordinary achievement by seemingly common people. It is also an account of unbelievable challenge and fierce adversity. And it is the story of a journey, of setting a course for the sun and, against all odds, of reaching it.

This is my account of the history of Sunrider and the lives of Tei Fu and Oi-Lin Chen. It is what I have both seen and what I know. I am well aware of my limitations, especially as a writer. Nevertheless, I feel a great need to tell the Sunrider story from my perspective. Perhaps my account of the lives of Tei Fu and Oi-Lin Chen, and the company they have built for nearly twenty years, can restore a measure of balance to the scales of justice. Perhaps to those millions of people whose lives have been or will be affected by Sunrider, my telling of the Sunrider story can enhance their journey in pursuit of health . . . of prosperity . . . of truth.

CHAPTER ONE

Worlds
Apart

The lives of Tei Fu Chen and Oi-Lin Tsui are a study in contrasts, not unlike the stark differences in their native countries.

In the small farming community of Chia Yi on the southwest side of the island of Taiwan, there is a dirt road. In 1948, despite the fact that nearly 20,000 people lived in Chia Yi, all the streets were dirt roads. They were all that was necessary. Following World War II, on the entire island of Taiwan there were few automobiles. In a rural community like Chia Yi, far from the capital city of Taipei, few people had ever seen a car, much less dreamed of owning one. If you were reasonably wealthy, you might hope to someday have a bicycle, which was a symbol of prosperity.

Walking was the norm in Chia Yi. Walking to the pineapple, sweet potato, and tobacco fields. Walking to the sugar mills, the distilleries, and the saw mills. Walking behind the water buffalo as it plowed through the rice paddies. And walking behind your parents, because that's what children do.

For the farmers, factory workers and children of Chia Yi, on foot was the only way to get where you were going. And most who lived in this small, undeveloped rural community were going nowhere.

Fifty-one years ago, when Tei Fu was born in his grandfather's home in Chia Yi County in the small town of Pu-Jsu, Taiwan was much different than today. Then it was backward—almost primitive—except for the few large cities like Taipei. People lived as they had for hundreds of generations. Like mainland China, Taiwan has a rich history of

Chinese culture and tradition. Order was well established in China, in Chia Yi, and in the Chen home.

Taiwan is a land of lush and rugged beauty. Fertile valleys of rich alluvial soil stand at the base of steep majestic mountains. The island is small—stretching only about 250 miles long and 80 miles wide at its widest point—and is shaped like a tobacco leaf. Where the land is too steep for farming, thick forests of cedar, rattan, oak, and camphor grow. Straddling the Tropic of Cancer, Taiwan is rich not only in beauty but in abundance of natural resources.

The Chinese and Japanese, the Dutch, the British, and the Spanish have all conquered and ruled Taiwan. It has been home to farmers and fishermen, pirates and political exiles. Until World War II, Japan had ruled the "Beautiful Island" for half a century. The Japanese occupation was oppressive and bitter for the native Chinese who primarily inhabited Taiwan. Japan attempted to remold the Chinese culture, and to force a severance of ancient Chinese roots, but was forced to surrender the island in 1945. Along with the Japanese failure of World War II, Chinese culture and tradition remained firmly intact in Taiwan.

Chiang Kai-Shjek was elected president of the Republic of China in 1948. His campaign against the Chinese Communists was failing, however. On December 7, 1949, when Tei Fu Chen was one year old, the Republic's government was forced to move its headquarters to Taipei. Subsequent defeat on mainland China resulted in millions of Nationalists fleeing across the Formosa Strait to make a new home on the tiny island.

Today, the Taiwanese hail from each of the primary

mainland provinces. The population has mushroomed over the past fifty years from eight million people to over twenty million. Entrepreneurial skills, combined with love of enterprise, have created a modern and thriving Taiwanese economy, one of the "four tigers" of the Pacific Rim.

In the early 1950s, Tei Fu had no idea of the volatility of the world he lived in. Chia Yi was quiet. It was removed, a world apart. His parents, like most married children who awaited the birth of their first child, lived with his father, along with many other Chen family members and in-laws. Tei Fu's father was named Yung-Yeuan Chen and his mother, Huang Lan.

The grandfather was the patriarch—a farmer, and blacksmith who hammered wagon wheels. His house was built in the very old Japanese style—a two-story house surrounded by rice fields. It had few rooms and a dirt floor. The ancient bathroom had no running water and an old wooden bathtub; the toilet had no "flush"—you simply squatted to do your business and once a week the refuse was collected and hauled away.

A wood-burning stove doubled as a water heater. The stove heated the water to prepare for the birth of a grandson. Children were born at home and there was no money for doctors or medicine. Following his successful delivery, Tei Fu's mother was given a rare treat by the grandfather—a small piece of fish.

The name given the new arrival, Tei Fu, means "gain wealth." Tei Fu's father, who had held a low-paying government job for the local Bureau of Tobacco since age seventeen, bestowed the tag on his firstborn son knowing there was little hope that the dream of wealth would ever be realized for himself.

According to Chinese custom, sons live with parents even after they are married. Typically they don't move out until a period after the first boy is born. Tei Fu's parents had been married and lived in the grandfather's home for over two years before he was born. They stayed with Tei Fu's grandfather for another two years after his birth. The rent was not cheap. Every month, Tei Fu's father surrendered his entire paycheck to his own father, as was the tradition for an "obedient son." To do less was to dishonor his father, and the Chen family name.

Grandpa Chen's house in Chia Yi was not his only home. His second small house was on the Pescadores Islands west of Taiwan in a village called Peng Hu. The home was not a luxury but a necessity. If a man was to have two wives, he needed two houses.

Polygamy was a common practice among many Chinese just a few generations ago. The more wives a man had, the greater the likelihood of having sons. The more sons a father had, the greater the chance he would be provided for, in middle age as well as old age. The grandchildren did not call their grandmothers by name. Grandpa Chen's first wife was called "Big Wife." His second wife, Tei Fu's paternal grandmother, was "Little Wife." Both wives bore sons. Big Wife had three daughters and one son, named Yuang Tan Chen. Little Wife had three daughters and two sons, of which Tei Fu's father Yung-Yeuan was the oldest. The two oldest sons called each other "brother," even though they had different mothers.

Perhaps it was never intended by Grandfather Chen, but fierce rivalry grew between his two families. At the forefront of the competition were the two oldest sons—Tei Fu's father and Tei Fu's uncle, Yuang Tan. If obedience was the measure, Yung-Yeuan was far more the "filial son." If monetary success was the standard, Tei Fu's uncle won hands down.

Yuang Tan had discovered a walkie-talkie, left on the island after World War II. It became the object of his fascination and ultimately his ticket to success. Using the abandoned object as a model, he founded his own electronics company and made millions of dollars. Unlike his brother, Yuang Tan did not feel an obligation to support his father or other family members. If Yung-Yeuan wanted to give their father his monthly paycheck, that was his decision. Besides, Yung-Yeuan, the low-level government worker, lived with their father. His small paycheck was not much to sacrifice, rationalized Yuang Tan.

If life as the under-achiever of two brothers was hard, the hardship was borne by Tei Fu's mother more than anyone. Huang Lan cooked, cleaned, and managed a household of ten to fifteen people, all crammed into a three-room house. She arose early to be first in line for the waste products from a tofu factory—the only food available for the family pig. She cooked over a wood-burning stove, even in the stifling humid heat of summer. She had to look after her own children, as well as in-laws who were living under their common roof. Huang Lan's life was hard . . . and hard she became.

There was no expectation of a Prince Charming who

would deliver Huang Lan from her Cinderella-like servitude. Her husband was a good man, but unlike his brother he would never be wealthy. Perhaps, she mused, there was a way her dreams could be realized *through her son*! Though she couldn't envision it at the time —still seeing women in their traditional subservient roles—her youngest *daughter* would eventually be the vehicle to vicarious fulfillment of her dreams, not her son. But it would be years before such a daughter was to be born. The hard life was here and now.

If one wanted to escape the dismal life in Chia Yi in the 1950s, the nearest big city with a thriving, robust economy was not Taipei to the north but Hong Kong, a few hundred miles to the west. Separating Chia Yi and Hong Kong is a narrow strait of water connecting the North and South China Seas. The actual distance between the cities is short, but at the time of Chen's youth, Hong Kong and Chia Yi were, in every sense, worlds apart.

It has been said if you visit Hong Kong just once, it is a city you will fall in love with at first sight, much like San Francisco or Paris. First impressions of Hong Kong may have more to do with sound than sight. It is a bustling, boisterous city with the pounding of jack-hammers, the honking of clogged traffic, and the hawking of street vendors. All the noises of a big city . . . the cacophony of an urban orchestra.

Hong Kong appeals to all of one's senses. Breathtaking harbor views coupled with the smell of fancy dim-sum—savory dumplings. Flashing neon lights and the gentle hum of Rolls Royces. Street vendor carts steaming with the sweet fragrances of shrimp wonton and noodles. Double-decker buses, chattering students in uniform, moss-green tennis courts, and groomed polo fields.

For most of the past 100 years, Hong Kong, Kowloon, and the New Territories have been under British control, and British influence is obvious everywhere. But the British presence finally came to an end. In 1997, Hong Kong reverted back to the control of the mainland Chinese government.

Trade is the lifeblood of the Hong Kong metropolis, and for decades this busy port city has been the lifeline of commerce to the mainland. With over 100 ships arriving each day, Hong Kong is one of the most vibrant ports in the world.

Along with the daily arrival of ships, trains, and airplanes, thousands of aliens flock to Hong Kong, some legally and some not. In the autumn of 1950, when Oi-Lin Tsui was born in a suburb of the New Territories called Fan Ling, the population of Hong Kong was about two million. Today, over six million people are crowded into this city that never seems to sleep. Skyscrapers stand shoulder-to-shoulder for miles in a continuous wall that gleams in the evening harbor lights.

One wonders where the millions find places to sleep at night. Housing is not a worry for the wealthy, and Hong Kong has more billionaires than any city in the world. Not all who come to Hong Kong come by way of wealth, however. Oi-Lin's family was typical of many Chinese families who lived in Hong Kong during the 1950s and '60s.

Oi-Lin's father was a talented engineer and her grandfather had been working in America for nearly twenty years. Upon the grandfather's return to Hong Kong, just before World War II, he used his savings to build their home in Fan Ling which provided a comfortable existence for Oi-Lin, the eldest of four children—two daughters and two sons.

Oi-Lin's mother suffered from severe mental illness and required lengthy treatments and institutionalization. Despite her mother's illness, home life was stable and good. With Oi-Lin and her grandmother supporting her father in rearing the family, the Tsui family existence was calm, simple, traditional, and conducive to a strong sense of self-worth.

As the oldest sibling, and with the burden of responsibility she felt compelled to bear, Oi-Lin became a serious person who matured much faster than her years. She naturally excelled in any assignment she undertook, especially as a student. Like her father, she had an exacting mind. Classmates could not keep up with her in math and science. English studies were mandatory, and were usually her least favorite subject. Still, given the British influences and living in a cosmopolitan city like Hong Kong, Oi-Lin's view of the world developed a distinct western flavor, coupled with a conviction that the world of her future would be driven by modern technology.

Oi-Lin's intelligence and independence made her feel that her destiny was in her hands. Of one thing she was certain: Her journey through life would not follow a typical path, nor would it be along dirt roads.

CHAPTER TWO

Tradition

$\mathcal{T}$he Chinese believe that happiness is learned by attending the classroom of the Creator—Mother Earth. Observe nature. Imitate nature. Learn from nature's model. Of all the laws of nature and the universe, perhaps the most basic are those that establish order. In both nature and society, order in all things is required to prevent chaos. Any time animals or humans choose to live together, order is established. When order is lost, civilizations are destroyed.

In every corner of nature, one can observe and learn the processes of order. In a pack of wolves, for example, there is an alpha wolf who is typically the largest, smartest, and most aggressive. The alpha wolf is the leader. He eats first, reproduces with the females, and bears the responsibility of leading the pack. After the alpha, rank is established among the other males and females. Age, size, health, ability, and personality typically determine who is submissive and who is dominant. The order may be periodically challenged, but it is also reaffirmed each day whenever the pack gathers. The wolves approach one another, some with ears, hair, and tails high as others cower with their tails tucked between their legs. Their behaviors signify their willingness to assume their earned roles. With order well-defined, the wolves have the best opportunity to survive, to create new generations, and to prosper as a pack.

Order in the human family obviously is far more complicated, but is just as real. Family order, once defined, is also reaffirmed on a daily basis. The family becomes the basic building block where rules of order for mankind are established. Families that live together and function in communities create societies. Communities that share stability and commonality over time are forged into states and nations.

For any nation to endure through centuries is rare. History teaches us that most empires rise and eventually fall. Struggles to revolutionize the class structure and order within a particular civilization typically precede the fall.

America, which is barely two centuries old, is perceived as a great nation. In fact, we are a very young and inexperienced society. The society of the Chinese, on the other hand, has endured through both centuries and millennia.

There is much to be learned about the rules of order from a nation that has not only survived but has dramatically progressed for a period of nearly 5,000 years. In Chinese society, it is not the largest, or smartest, or most aggressive wolf who is the alpha. That rank is bestowed automatically to the father.

While most Chinese observe either the Buddhist religion or Taoism, it is the Chinese *culture* and *traditions* that have endured the test of time and that have been the glue holding together that great civilization for over fifty centuries. China is a country of great ethnic and religious diversity. While Buddhism, Taoism, Christianity, Islam and many other formal religions have existed for centuries in China, the teachings of the great philosophers predominantly have directed much of the Asian social and political development.

Of all of the great schools of thought that course through Chinese history, it was Confucius (551–479 B.C.) who taught the basic order and rules of everyday life. Confucian ethics are the single most important dynamic in the lives of both the Taiwanese and the mainland Chinese people. Confucius' writings constitute the Chinese gospel. Confucius did not teach religion so much as he did a value system whereby families, communities, and nations could survive and prosper.

Confucius taught that there was no greater value than maintaining harmony in the world, and that every person has their individual place and role in society. If individuals and families could observe established rules of social behavior and order, harmony for all would result.

Order, according to Confucius, was established as follows:

> First and foremost, a person should be a loyal subject to their ruler
> Secondly, a son should obey his father
> Third, a younger brother should defer to an older brother
> Fourth, a wife should support her husband
> Fifth, friends should practice loyalty to one another

Loyalty, respect, and obedience are integral dynamics in Chinese relationships. Good relationships, as well as the observance of order, will inevitably result in harmony within society. Through thousands of years, Chinese children have been brought up to respect the family structure, told that they owe their primary duty first and foremost to the family. Families who observe "filial piety" are perpetuated and create the basic stability for both the individual and the family. According to Confucius, "Filial piety is the root of all virtue, and that from which all teaching comes."

"Our bodies in every hair and bit of skin are received by us from our parents, and we must not venture to injure or scar them." Confucius taught that obedience and respect for parents is the core virtue from which all others flow. Death is a better alternative than to bring hurt or shame upon one's parents. Properly observed, filial piety creates in an individual integrity, propriety, righteousness, and the fundamental establishment of one's personality.

Respect and obedience to one's elders is a tradition observed not just by the Chinese—it is followed by peoples throughout Asia. And certainly it was the order established in the home in which Tei Fu Chen was reared. Tei Fu's father respected, honored, and obeyed his own father. Tei Fu's mother was submissive to her husband. Tei Fu was taught, especially as the oldest son, that his primary duty in life was to honor his parents by *obeying* them.

The code of conduct prescribed by Confucius 2,500 years ago was the primary discipline in Chen's childhood upbringing. It would continue through his adult life. Tei Fu Chen as the *filial son*. It was the standard by which his parents would judge him . . . and one day reject him. It was *the issue* with which he would struggle desperately throughout his entire life. His search would result more often in questions than answers.

Ultimately, answers would be found. They would come, however, not from the books of Confucius but from the voices in Chen's heart.

∾

Traditionally, Chinese sons are more cherished than daughters because they carry on the family name and perform the filial role of protecting and providing for elderly parents. Beyond the monetary and practical issues of providing parents with "social security," the Chinese are taught from youth that the most important way they can honor and respect their parents and their heritage is by how they project the family "face" in society.

In the hierarchy of Chinese core family values, the concept of "keeping face" is a value equally as important as "filial piety." These two values travel hand-in-hand and complement each other. In part, it is the idea of upholding a person's and a family's prestige in society. In part, it's a matter of an individual's integrity.

Americans tend to think of "saving face" as a simple matter of appearance or avoiding embarrassment. To the Chinese, face is a far deeper issue. It is how one projects their sense of self-worth. Face is demonstrated through your status in society, level of education, the nature of your job, your ancestry, and your personal accomplishments. Face is also how an individual honors his or her parents, and the society in which they live. Chinese culture is based upon face and its opposing characteristic, "shame." Success brings face. Failure brings shame.

The concepts of filial piety and face are inseparable. To honor and respect one's family maintains face. To rebel or disobey one's parents results in the losing of face. Losing face results in shame. Both face and shame are projected not

just on individuals, but also upon their families. Shaming
yourself and/or your parents is to shame society. Society
rejects those who shame it. There is no worse fate . . . not
even death.

CHAPTER THREE

The
Filial
Son

$\mathcal{I}$n Taiwan and China as through much of Asian culture, having a good education is considered the top personal priority. A great majority of young people grow up in meager and difficult circumstances. An education is their only ticket to a more hopeful future. Parents put great pressure on their children to study hard. The Chinese system of education is designed to filter out the weak and mediocre and give opportunity only to those with native intelligence who are diligent in their pursuits. Motivation is most often achieved through shame, fear, or in the case of Tei Fu Chen, physical punishment.

Papa Chen felt the best approach was the "can and the stick." When Tei Fu would return home with his report card, which consistently indicated a lack of performance, Papa Chen would respond by putting a can on a stick and repeatedly striking his son, hoping he would get the message that bad grades were unacceptable in the Chen home. Tei Fu dreaded the whippings. Still, he lacked the motivation to be a good student. In his school, if test scores were over 60 percent, one passed. Anything under 60 was automatic failure. And for most of the time that he was in elementary school, Tei Fu failed to receive passing grades. Of the seventy-three children in his fifth grade class, only one received a grade lower than Tei Fu.

Perhaps Papa Chen's pressure tactics would have been more effective had father and son spent more time together. But Tei Fu has no memory of sharing with his father leisurely walks, baseball games, soccer games, or for that matter any other bonding experience. In 1950s' Taiwan, the focus was on *survival*. The law of the family was obedience. If a son was uneducated, it was the father who was to blame.

There was virtually no communication between father and son. While most families sit around the dinner table and talk about the day's activities, in the Chen household the children were not allowed to talk during the meal. The only opportunity for them to speak came after dinner. And then the only interest of the father was on his son's activities at school that day. Invariably, those reports were followed by the nightly punishment.

There were other reasons that Tei Fu struggled in school. The teachers were poorly paid. Most of them earned a second income by tutoring their students outside of the classroom. Parents who paid the teachers extra money found that their children received extra attention in school. But Papa Chen had no spare money for tutors, so Tei Fu's teachers had no added incentive to spend extra time with him or other failing students from poor families.

When Tei Fu was at home there were no real distractions to keep him from his studies. There was no TV, radio, or newspaper. No games or toys to divert his attention. His mind constantly wandered, however. He spent his time daydreaming. Dreaming of worlds across the ocean. Dreaming of being rich or famous. The young and immature Tei Fu could not comprehend that education would be his ticket to the life of his dreams.

Belying his marks in school, Tei Fu was very bright, though he found most of his classes and textbooks quite boring. He loved to read. Hours on end were spent in the library or at neighborhood bookstores reading what he found intriguing. His favorite subject wasn't sports. It wasn't world travel. It was philosophy and history. Compared to most boys his age, he was odd indeed!

Of the period spent in elementary school, Tei Fu did have one good year, the sixth grade. Finally he had a teacher who actually took an interest in him and made the effort to spend a little extra time with him. Even though he wasn't being paid as a tutor by the Chen family, in the school yard he went out of his way to be nice to Chen and encourage him to do well in his classes. Approval and encouragement were new to Tei Fu. He began spending more time studying his textbooks, not because he found them interesting, but because he sought the ongoing approval of a teacher who seemed to care. That year, primarily because of the encouragement of a single teacher, Tei Fu finished in the top ten in his class. He passed a difficult examination, enabling him to advance to the best junior high school in Chia Yi—a big hurdle for a bad student to jump.

With the opportunity for his son to advance, Papa Chen seemed pleased. The routine beatings came to an end. The next year, however, the old pattern was renewed. His new teachers showed little interest in Tei Fu and he reverted back to his old ways. Textbooks were ignored. Hours instead were devoted to Chinese history, Chinese culture, and the Chinese philosophies that had been 7,000 years in the making.

During most of his early life, Tei Fu was weak, skinny, and sickly. Neighborhood bullies called him *Tofu*. He became the target of their physical aggression and demeaning pranks. Often, walking to and from school, he was pushed, shoved, and otherwise humiliated. He became the butt of crude and insensitive jokes and taunting. Tei Fu had not yet learned that what is to be feared more than loss of blood is loss of self-respect. He made a point of going to school only on days when he could walk with his older sister, Sheue Wen. She was his protector and defender, and the bullies were less likely to pick on him when she was by his side.

The primary reason Chen was so sickly was because his diet consisted mostly of rice and sweet potatoes. Rarely was there any meat. His mother recognized the inadequacies in his diet and attempted to breast feed him until he was nearly six. Still, most of the time he felt ill, weakened with colds and allergies. Living in a house where chickens and ducks and dogs roamed freely also created an unsanitary and unhealthy living environment. Flu and diarrhea were common, for both Tei Fu and the chickens.

Tei Fu's parents didn't have money to take him to a doctor. The only person who concerned himself with Tei Fu's health was his Grandpa Chen. The grandfather believed in the medicinal value of herbs. Whenever Tei Fu was ailing, the grandfather would boil a pot of water, put large quantities and varieties of herbs into the pot, and steep the concoction until it was a thick, bitter concentrated brew. The old man would then hold the little boy in his arms, pinch his nose, encourage him to open his mouth, and pour the thick liquid down his throat. Tei Fu hated the taste, but invariably the herbs seemed to work. After drinking his grandfather's herbal potions, he always seemed to feel stronger, and his illnesses at least temporarily would depart.

For most of Taiwan's post-World War II society, especially those who lived on farms, medicine was nearly impossible to come by. Herbs, on the other hand, were readily available. For Chinese of Tei Fu's generation, herbs were used to treat common ailments because herbs were all they had.

By the time Tei Fu was in school, his family had moved to a different city, about a fifty-minute bus ride from his grandfather's home. He loved to visit his grandfather, in part because his grandfather's herbs alleviated the symptoms of his allergies and illnesses, and in part because he found the herbal knowledge his grandfather had accumulated over a lifetime to be fascinating.

Another highlight of visiting Grandpa Chen was that he, unlike Tei Fu's parents, enjoyed delighting the children with treats of candy. To Tei Fu, a piece of candy was the highlight of his week. Both he and his sister Sheue Wen looked forward to their grandfather's sweet treats, especially during the Chinese New Year when Grandpa Chen rewarded his grandchildren with a few extra pieces. Typically when Tei Fu visited his grandfather, he would not leave until they ate dinner. At the dinner table sat the old man. He had no teeth and little facial hair, and what sparse strands he had were long and ungroomed. He ate slowly, savoring the soft, sticky rice called "mochi." Grandfather and grandson spent many hours together, Tei Fu harvesting a small portion of the knowledge the old man possessed. Then it was time for the sticky rice. To this day, mochi is still Tei Fu Chen's favorite food.

Chen remembers the day his grandfather died, at age seventy-five. After his death, Chen's father and his step-brothers split up what few meager belongings the grandfather had accumulated. During one of Chen's visits to his grandfather, Grandpa Chen had shown his grandson an old Chinese manuscript that contained much of his knowledge about herbs and herbal formulations. It was classic ancient Chinese literature, written in poetic verse. It was uniquely different from any textbook Chen had ever read as a student. Neither Chen's father nor uncles had an interest in the rare herbal book. Tei Fu took it home and eventually spent hours, days, and months studying its contents. The book contained the bases for many of the formulas upon which Sunrider's first and most popular products would be founded.

Chen remembers the day his grandfather died, at age seventy-five. After his death, Chen's father and his step-brothers split up what few meager belongings the grandfather had accumulated. During one of Chen's visits to his grandfather, Grandpa Chen had shown his grandson an old Chinese manuscript that contained much of his knowledge about herbs and herbal formulations. It was classic ancient Chinese literature, written in poetic verse. It was uniquely different from any textbook Chen had ever read as a student. Neither Chen's father nor uncles had an interest in the rare herbal book. Tei Fu took it home and eventually spent hours, days, and months studying its contents. The book contained the bases for many of the formulas upon which Sunrider's first and most popular products would be founded.

In the years that passed after Papa Chen moved out of his father's home and established a greater sense of independence, he began building a life that centered on his wife and children. He also began climbing the employment ladder. For the first time, he began making enough money to improve the standard of living for his family and to provide a measure of relief to the hard life that Tei Fu's mother had especially suffered. Papa Chen worked for the Bureau of Liquor and Cigarettes, then was employed by local Chia Yi County in their planning department. On weekends he also did freelance architecture, designing homes for what was becoming an emerging middle class in Taiwan. The second job brought in much-needed extra income, which he no longer shared completely with Grandpa Chen. Years later, he pursued real estate full time, buying and selling land and building spec homes.

The Chen family continued to grow with daughters. In 1954, Jau-Fang was born, followed by Jau-Hwa in 1957. Jau-Fei, born in 1962, was the last of the Chen children. Beautiful even as a baby, she was to be the "darling" of the family. Tei Fu's parents had desperately hoped to have another boy, but after four daughters and one son, they felt they could not support a larger family. Tei Fu remained closest to his older sister, Sheue Wen. The three younger girls grew close to one another, even though their parents obviously favored the youngest, Jau-Fei. If the dreams of the parents were not to be lived through the oldest son, perhaps they could be realized through the youngest daughter.

As Papa Chen's real estate business flourished, the Chens were able to move into one of the spec homes that he had built. It was a dramatic departure from the homes in which Tei Fu was born and initially reared. The new home was small, but clean and modern. Instead of sharing one bedroom that doubled as a kitchen, the new home had three bedrooms. Barnyard animals were not allowed inside the home, or outside in the tiny yard. There was even a toilet with running water.

Tei Fu was still very skinny. His family teased him by saying that he needed to walk slowly through the shower to even get wet. But the basic comforts of life in the new home gave Tei Fu a feeling of invigoration and a new, strange sense of self-worth. The Chen family still did not own a car, however. An automobile was neither a comfort nor a necessity.

"Someday," Chen resolved to himself, "I will own both a house and a car. And someday, I'll buy a car for my Mama and Papa."

He didn't know how—he just knew that someday he would.

CHAPTER FOUR

———————

Wisdom of the Ancients

As Chen entered his teenage years, he continued to face a variety of health challenges. His poor health was a direct result of inadequate nutrition in the food he ate. Even when he wasn't ill, he felt lacking in strength and energy. He continued to seek out and to be fascinated by the effects of his grandfather's herbal remedies. If herbs could have such a powerful impact in remedying his illnesses, he concluded they might also be effective in helping him maintain his health even when he wasn't ill. His curiosity became an obsession, and his obsession soon turned into passion. Chen began what would become a lifelong study of the concepts behind herbal health and nutrition.

His discovery was in a very real sense a journey—a journey backward through time. A journey through the books and manuscripts, some of which were thousands of years old, that contained the concepts of health and the philosophies of living long and living well. The books and manuscripts he studied contained truths based upon hundreds of generations of experience spread through thousands of years. Nowhere in the history of mankind was there a more comprehensive record of herbal philosophies as they related to health. As Chen became totally immersed in his study of the manuscripts, he learned many concepts and philosophies that seemed simple truths.

In the earliest days of man, long before there were medical doctors, the inhabitants of the planet considered many possibilities to cure their diseases and ailments. Every avenue was explored, including magic and sorcery, prayer, music, diet, rest, exercise, fresh air, and internal and external remedies that were prepared from plants, animals, and minerals. Of all of these approaches to health, plant remedies have been the most consistent form of treatment throughout the history of China.

Because ancient Chinese people and their rulers had no real belief or understanding of a life after death, their focus was on the quality of their present life. Their ambition was very simple—to live long and to live well. The most revered in these early societies were the temple priests. They served as both spiritual advisors to their leaders and as medicine men, experimenting constantly with herbs and plants to provide physical relief from injuries and disease.

Early in China's history, the kingdom was factionalized into many different regions, all separately ruled. Each society was comprised of a variety of craftsmen—farmers, hunters, soldiers, and priests who were skilled in the art of healing broken bones, injuries, and wounds. Each craft carefully recorded the rules and procedures with the intention of passing their wisdom and knowledge down to future generations.

The Chinese traditionally have had great respect for nature. They believed that God created Mother Earth with the expectation that nature would serve as the model for all human behavior. The universe consisted of three dimensions: heaven, man, and earth. The answers to mankind's existence could come from heaven or earth. In the absence of religion, Mother Nature became the teacher.

The ancient Chinese were the first to recognize that we literally are what we eat. Thousands of years ago, one ancient Chinese researcher named Sheng Nung took it upon himself to test, one by one, hundreds of different plants. He studied and recorded the effects on his body of as many as one hundred different plants and herbs a day. Methodically he recorded his findings and noted the effects of the various herbs and herbal formulations upon his body and health. His research came to a tragic end when he mixed a potion that created a deadly combination of herbs. Just as he had discovered the benefits of many herbs, he also discovered they can have very negative—even fatal—side effects.

Through his research, Sheng Nung became known as the God of Herbs. Some of the best known Chinese herbs today are traced back to Sheng Nung's discoveries, including such common herbs as cinnamon, citrus, ginger, ginseng, lotus seed, and rhubarb. Sheng Nung taught the Chinese how to identify, cultivate, care for and utilize plants and herbs to benefit the human body. More importantly, he discovered that the body could bring itself to a near-perfect state of health using the right plant combinations which would nourish the entire body.

That concept would become the foundation of the philosophy which was developed and refined over thousands of years, but which in modern time became largely lost or ignored. It was a philosophy of which Tei Fu Chen developed a deep understanding and conviction, and which he later would come to call the "Philosophy of Regeneration." The conviction that Tei Fu developed was simple: The human body is nearly perfect in its design. Man's creator fashioned his body to be self-governing, containing a variety of systems and organs that work in concert with one another, and that maintain an innate, natural ability to regulate systems such as blood pressure, blood sugar, and body temperature. Other than injury, health challenges occur when the body becomes out of balance. Chen believed, just as Sheng Nung held thousands of years before, that if a body is properly nourished and cleansed, harmony and balance will occur naturally. When in balance, the body can regulate and respond to any form of illness or health challenge. The Philosophy of Regeneration simply stated is this: *With proper nourishment, the human body has the power to heal and regulate itself, and maintain optimum health and peak performance.*

The ancient wise men and temple priests who advanced these simple truths thousands of years ago devoted lifetimes learning how to properly nourish the body so it could keep its proper balance. They experimented with thousands of different foods and food combinations to develop precise herbal formulas that could most completely nourish the human body, and remove from the body wastes and toxins that could otherwise disrupt natural balance.

The ancient health concepts and philosophies that Chen studied were even more far-reaching. Early doctors believed that instead of taking medicine to help cure a health problem, one should instead eat the proper herbs to prevent the body from ever getting sick. This health concept was not limited to the Chinese. Even Hippocrates, 400 B.C., said, "Let food be your medicine, and medicine be your food."

In the ancient Chinese way of thinking, hunger and disease were very much related—left unattended, both resulted in poor health and imbalance. Illness often meant that the body "hungered," or lacked nutrition. Those systems that suffered most from malnourishment ceased to function properly, creating imbalance and subsequent illness or disease.

When Huang Ti, also known as the "Yellow Emperor," began his rule approximately 4,600 years ago, he assembled an elite group of Chinese doctors and charged them to discover the secrets of life, health, and vitality for himself and his family.

Chi Po, one of his ministers, was appointed to taste and experiment with herbs and plants and to continue the pioneering efforts of Sheng Nung. These processes would ultimately continue for thousands of years through the Ming Dynasty, which lasted from A.D. 1368 through 1664. The study of herbs evolved into both an art and science. Near the end of the Ming Dynasty, a naturalist named Li Shih Chen produced a landmark manuscript entitled *Pen Tsao Kang Mu* which translated is the *Catalog of Medicinal Herbs.* This manuscript contained formulas for over 2,000 varieties of herbs and was the most comprehensive assemblage of herbal formulations in the history of humankind.

Many of these ancient documents were carved in wood or bone and are extant. From these ancient carvings and writings emerged not only the principles of the Philosophy of Regeneration, but also many of the fundamental philosophies and concepts that became the foundation for modern internal medicine. An untitled Chinese manuscript written 400 years ago became a historic turning point where health and medicine became less a practice of tradition and much more a direct scientific approach.

While the Chinese were the first to discover the actual healing power of herbs, many other civilizations went through their own processes of discovery. For example, nearly 3,000 years ago, the Egyptians used garlic, castor oil, coriander, mint and many other herbs for both food and medicine. Even the Old Testament mentions herbal usage and cultivation.

Meanwhile, in China the development of the Philosophy of Regeneration and the concepts of harmony and balance were almost lost nearly 2,200 years ago during a period known as the "Warring States." Before the great wars and seasons of discontent, doctors were trained to promote wellness. They were paid based upon their ability to maintain the health of their people. During this turbulent period in Chinese history, however, herbs were diverted from their traditional role as foods and instead used as poultices and cures by Chinese herbal doctors to treat wounds, injuries, and disease. This approach, also known as the "substitution," focused on treating symptoms rather than promoting wellness and prevention.

Following the Warring States, the study of herbs for nutritional purposes was largely abandoned. Many traditions survived, however. Even today herbs play a vital role in the Chinese approach to health. It is difficult to walk down any street in China or elsewhere in Asia without passing at least one herbal shop where a person typically can find several hundred herbs displayed on shelves. No informed person would disagree that when it comes to an understanding of herbs and herbal nutrition, the Chinese have a culture and a history that far surpass any other culture or society.

CHAPTER FIVE

Yin
and
Yang

Hot and cold. Light and dark. Sweet and sour. Active and calm. Domineering and submissive. Male and female.

In America, we most often view paired opposites as mismatched. The western mind-set is more apt to see contrast than commonality.

Asian cultures are more inclined to see the matching of opposites in a constructive light. The Chinese term for paired opposites is *Yin and Yang*. Yin, the more female in character, represents the yielding, the calming, the submissive, the pulling, the shadow. Yang, the more male side, is active, aggressive, dynamic, pushing, and in the light. Everything in the universe contains elements of both Yin and Yang. A coin for example, has two sides. The side facing the light will be illuminated—the other side will be in the shadow.

Water is another example. Because it is yielding in nature, it represents the Yin. However, over time, even the rigid face of the Earth, a Yang element, yields to the predictable motion of the water.

Neither the Yin nor the Yang is more important than the other. Symbolically, they are identical in shape, but opposite in color. Looking like a pair of curved tadpoles, when united as one, the Yin and Yang form a perfect circle—a universe all their own. Ultimately, the concept of Yin and Yang is reduced to the most basic law of the universe: Yin and Yang are designed to create *balance,* and from balance comes *life.*

The Chinese refer to the essence of all things living as

"qi" or "chi," which is divided into two forces, the Yin and Yang. The breath, then, is the Chi, while inhaling is Yin and exhaling is Yang. The Chinese view of life, and of all things in nature, is predicated upon the simple, yet beautiful concepts of Yin and Yang.

Food is both categorized and prepared according to the Yin and Yang philosophy. After all, food is necessary to all living things. We are what we eat. And most of us eat several times a day. Yang, or "hot" foods, stimulate the body and deplete energy; while Yin foods are "cool" and nourish, calm, and re-energize. "Neutral" foods which are both Yin and Yang are balanced and create balance.

Every Chinese food dish is prepared with balance in mind. Americans may think of Chinese food in terms of "sweet and sour," but in reality tens of thousands of Chinese food dishes have been created, all with the purpose of achieving *balance.* Chinese chefs are masters of the art form of Yin and Yang; and as with any master, are said to have "good kung fu."

The Yin and Yang concept is further developed when considering the means whereby health can be achieved in the human body. A person "in balance" is healthy. When balance is lost, good health suffers. Blood pressure can be too high (hypertension) or too low (hypotension). Emotions can have too much anxiety-producing Yang, or be depressed because the Yin element is out of balance. In a healthy immune system Yin resists infection by providing the defense. An overly aggressive Yang goes on the offensive in attacking allergens which result in allergies. The simple concepts of balance and health in the human body can become quite complicated when one considers thousands of foods and hundreds of body parts and systems.

Yin and Yang is a concept of balance—in nature, in humans, and in relationships. In many respects, Tei Fu and Oi-Lin were paired opposites. Oi-Lin was the pragmatist, the mathematician, the even-keeled. Tei Fu was the philosopher, the dreamer, the artist. Oi-Lin was beautiful and refined. Tei Fu was skinny and awkward. Oi-Lin was the scientist who saw a modern world; Tei Fu was the traditionalist who believed in the wisdom of the ancients.

For all of their differences, there were also many similarities. Both were very independent and non-conformist. Both were hard-working, humble people who shared a dream of a profession where they could be care-givers.

Their common dreams brought them to the same place, at the same time—Kaoshiung Medical College. Their motivations in becoming medical doctors were not the same. Tei Fu's ambition to be a doctor was born of his parents. Oi-Lin's motivation was born of her heart.

While it was their differences that attracted them to one another from their first meeting, it was what they held in common that would one day bond them tightly together as a couple.

The highest honor in the Asian culture is to have a son become either a doctor or professor. These are considered the most prestigious and well-paying jobs that honor the parents and ensure the ability to take care of them as they grow old. As Tei Fu began high school, both parents encouraged him to become a doctor. He could bring great pride and acclaim to the family. Tei Fu was easily persuaded.

He had grown up sickly, and the thought of being able to treat and help others had great appeal. But studying math and science was less appealing; his first love was still the study of herbs and Chinese philosophy and history. Nevertheless, in 1968 he applied to Kaoshiung Medical College and was accepted. His parents were delighted—until they found out his grades were not good enough to get into the regular medical program. Instead he chose pharmacy as his major. Still, having a son in medical school was a source of great pride to Mama and Papa Chen.

Meanwhile, in Hong Kong, Oi-Lin Tsui also had a dream to attend medical school. Unlike Tei Fu, Oi-Lin loved the math and science classes that she had taken for most of her life. In most respects she was much like her father—quiet, studious, and precise. She had little interest in the philosophies and traditions of the past. Growing up in bustling Hong Kong, Oi-Lin had had much exposure to the new world of science and modern technology. She was quite shy, but very much a people person. In playing a large role in rearing her younger brothers and sister, Oi-Lin had become a skilled nurturer. She felt being a medical doctor would give her the opportunity to help others through her pursuit of modern science.

Kaoshiung, home to the medical college, is the second largest city in Taiwan and the country's primary seaport. Over one and a half million people live in Kaoshiung today. Located about two hours south of Tei Fu's birthplace of Chia Yi, Kaoshiung became Tei Fu's first exposure to life in a large city. Kaoshiung is very crowded and traffic and noise are constant. Unlike the more agrarian environment where he had been raised, Kaoshiung seemed dirty and the air polluted. While Tei Fu was fascinated with the bustling city and the prospect of medical school, he worried that the dirty air would affect his allergies and encourage his sickly state.

When Oi-Lin received the letter informing her that she had been accepted to Kaoshiung Medical College, the least of her worries was the challenge of living in a crowded, busy city like Kaoshiung. The fact that she did not speak Mandarin—the language in which her classes would be taught— was not an issue either, even though Cantonese, Oi-Lin's native language, bore little resemblance even to Taiwanese, a dialect much more like Mandarin. So in September 1968 when Oi-Lin was nearly eighteen years old, she left Hong Kong in pursuit of a dream and an ambition she had held throughout her life.

Along with two high school friends who had also been accepted into medical school, Oi-Lin boarded a large old boat and began her journey to a new country. Although the distance was not great, the ride across the Formosa Strait seemed to take forever. Nevertheless, there was a great feeling of adventure among the three friends. After two days on the boat and a couple of hours in a car, they arrived in Taipei, where their spirit of adventure was dampened somewhat in learning that they still had a nine-hour train ride from Taipei to Kaoshiung. Unfortunately the night train was typically jammed with passengers, leaving no room for them to sit; so standing and holding their bags, they suffered through the long ride to Kaoshiung. There they moved into a small room they previously had arranged to rent in someone's home.

Some of Oi-Lin's friends saw the adventure not so much as an opportunity to become medical doctors but as the perfect place *to find a husband* who was likely to become a medical doctor. Oi-Lin, on the other hand, by nature was studious and fiercely independent. Not only was she *not* looking for a husband, Oi-Lin had never even dated someone seriously. Her dream was crystal clear and etched in her soul. She *would* become a medical doctor. She *would* overcome the language barrier. And *nothing* would stand in her way.

❧

As a student in medical school, Tei Fu continued to struggle but squeezed by.

"If you could just get these two questions right, you could easily pass," a professor said to him one day, trying to encourage Tei Fu to study a little more diligently. As he spoke, a young attractive student walked by. "Look at that girl," added the professor, nodding at Oi-Lin, "She can't even speak Mandarin, and yet she consistently scores the top grades in the class."

Tei Fu had noticed Oi-Lin before but did not realize she did not speak Mandarin. It did not surprise him that she was an excellent student—she *looked* smart! It was October 1969 and Oi-Lin was a nineteen-year-old sophomore. Tei Fu was twenty-one years old.

Both for extra credit and recreation, he taught a folk dance class. Chen was pleased that Oi-Lin was one of the students in the class. One day he approached her and offered to help teach her an easy dance. She looked at him quizzically, wondering why he hadn't chosen someone else to teach. Tei Fu charmed her by saying, "I was waiting for you." After the first dance, he asked her for a second. And after the second dance he mustered the courage to ask her out on a date.

Tei Fu impressed Oi-Lin from the start. "I like people who aren't shy. And Tei Fu wasn't shy at all," Oi-Lin says of her first impression. "Many of the Chinese boys at the college were shy and lacking in confidence. And even though Tei Fu was skinnier than most of the others, he had a very confident and easy way. Plus, I thought he was very handsome. At least he had the potential to be!"

Oi-Lin sat behind Tei Fu on his Yamaha motorcycle as they weaved their way through traffic into downtown Kaoshiung. It was their first date. They split a tall glass of papaya milk and then went bowling, also a first for both of them.

Bowling was not the only new experience. Neither Tei Fu nor Oi-Lin had ever before dated anyone seriously. Neither was experienced in the courting process and both had difficulty understanding the other's language. Silence between them was common, but never awkward. They just enjoyed spending time together.

Tei Fu learned that Oi-Lin was in the judo club, so he joined as well. He was somewhat embarrassed participating in sports because he was so skinny and felt comparatively weak and out of shape. An anatomy teacher once commented to him, "If you don't remember how many bones are in your body, just touch yourself, you should be able to recognize most of them."

To add some meat to those bones, Tei Fu did what he had always done when looking for health solutions—find the right combination of herbs that could give him more energy and help him become stronger. Ever since his grandfather's death, Tei Fu had been forced to turn to the books and manuscripts that herbal mentors had written. Tei Fu no longer viewed herbs just as treatment for illness. He had studied the herbal traditions deeply enough to realize that herbs had much greater value than simply to be smelly, bitter concoctions to remedy an illness.

Chen had great respect for the powers of nature to promote health and strength. He began to study herbs more diligently than ever. He sought and continually ate the herbs his ancestors had found through generations of time were most effective. To properly nourish and strengthen his body, he showed much greater care in everything he ate and became more disciplined in exercising and in developing the capacities of each of his body systems.

Before long, Chen began to bulk-up and his friends no longer joked about his physique. With broad, well-muscled shoulders and a thin waist, he looked healthy—even athletic. He excelled at judo as well as other Chinese martial arts. Eventually he could do over 400 pushups without a break. As his body strengthened, he advanced to karate and then to tae kwon do and won many black belts and tournament championships. Besides Tei Fu's strong physique, his instructors attributed his success to a "kick that wouldn't quit." That gusto would follow him through life.

Tei Fu looked much better. Feeling a true sense of health for the first time in his life, his self-confidence also grew dramatically. He smiled whenever he saw the cartoon character Popeye, who opens his ever-ready can of spinach each time he needs to accomplish some Herculean feat. Tei Fu felt like a Chinese Popeye because of the obvious effect the herbs had upon his health, his strength, and his ability to succeed.

Despite the dramatic changes in Chen's appearance, most other medical students, including Oi-Lin, felt that Chen's preoccupation with herbs was generally misguided. Tremendous advances had been made in the world of medicine. Western discoveries and inventions were advancing so rapidly that even the most aggressive students had difficulty comprehending all the new facets and emerging opportunities of modern medicine. Why did Chen continue to focus primarily upon the ancient and traditional rather than the new and modern? Who would choose the past, and in the process give up such an intriguing future?

Tei Fu and Oi-Lin had many deep and heartfelt discussions about concepts of health and the new versus the old. Occasionally they argued, but mostly they learned a great deal from one another and achieved new respect for each other's background, value system, and paradigm of the world. They shared much more in common than they realized. Their differences seemed to complement rather than conflict with one another. "We were the perfect Yin-Yang match," Oi-Lin concluded. "Different, but very much alike. And when together, made whole."

Once he felt confident in Oi-Lin's respect and trust, Tei Fu disclosed another part of his life that was profoundly important to him but which few people could understand or accept. Tei Fu had deeply rooted religious beliefs.

As with most Taiwanese, Tei Fu was brought up with the philosophies of Buddhism and Taoism. But neither he nor his family ever practiced a formal religion. He was searching for a religion in which he could believe. His first introduction to organized religion was when he was in high school and met a pair of young missionaries of the Mormon Church (formally The Church of Jesus Christ of Latter-day Saints, or LDS). They were two of the first four missionaries in Chia Yi. Tei Fu loved to learn about philosophy and was intrigued to know what motivated those young men to spend two years of their lives as volunteers teaching other people about their religion. Over much time and many discussions, Tei Fu not only learned about the LDS religion, but also came to embrace the basic principles of Christianity.

In his Chinese culture, he was taught to worship both ancestors and God. History books and manuscripts had taught him a great deal about his ancestors. But Tei Fu had no real comprehension of the nature of God. Just as he had always sought the love and approval of his own father, in his soul he knew he had a Heavenly Father, a being who had created his spirit, just as his mortal parents had created his body.

The missionaries taught Tei Fu the LDS beliefs about God—that every person has a Heavenly Father who knows them and cares for them individually, and who has created them—His children—for an eternal purpose. The missionaries shared the Mormon views of a pre-mortal existence, of

the purposes of this life, and of what awaits us after we die.
Tei Fu liked the Mormon belief that the basic doctrines of
the gospel are contained within the Bible, but that God's
children don't need to rely upon the Bible alone for divine
guidance. At the head of the LDS Church is a prophet who
directs the affairs of the Church, and who Mormons believe
receives divine inspiration and revelation, even today. It
made such sense to Tei Fu. If God is dead, why worship a
dead man? And if he is living, would he not want to share
his wisdom and love on an ongoing basis?

Tei Fu was also passionate about learning the teachings
of Jesus Christ. He was impressed that when Jesus chose his
twelve apostles, he picked ordinary people. The LDS
Church seemed to be a religion for all people, not just the
wealthy or the accomplished. Tei Fu attended church services and felt welcomed and accepted. He felt a sense of
family and a sense of worth.

Learning the LDS beliefs also enabled Chen to view
Confucius and his philosophies in a whole new light. Life
should be more than just the pragmatic rules of Confucius
or the philosophies of a few great men. The freedom to
think and to garner wisdom is not limited to just a few, but
is the option of everyone.

One other LDS teaching that particularly impressed the
teenage mind of Tei Fu Chen was the concept of agency,
that the greatest gift God has given His children is their
ability to make choices. "We have the freedom to choose,"
Chen was taught. "We can choose right or we can choose
wrong. What we can't change is truth—and that there will
always be consequences for our actions." After studying

with the missionaries and praying hard to know the truth of their message, Tei Fu decided to convert to the Mormon religion—something extraordinary for a Taiwanese youth to do. Tei Fu also chose not to tell his parents about his conversion. They had a rigid standard to which he was expected to conform, and he knew they would be bitterly disappointed in him for choosing a way that was not theirs. Every Sunday, to attend church, he would leave home, simply telling his parents that he was going out to find some peace.

Tei Fu's nonconformity to Chinese expectations was a great challenge to Oi-Lin. Her friends constantly asked, "Why do you date someone who has such strange views? Why do you have a relationship with someone who will likely become a pharmacist while you become a medical doctor?" Her friends could not understand why Oi-Lin would consider being with a man whose life's star seemed fixed much lower in the galaxy than her own. The concept of "face" in the Chinese culture is especially deep when considering a mate.

CHAPTER SIX

Two Become One

*T*ei Fu barely had enough money to pay for school and living expenses. Dates with Oi-Lin were mostly a much-anticipated opportunity to spend time together. Oi-Lin would accompany Tei Fu during his research projects for school. They would often ride his motor scooter up into the mountains to pick herbs.

Tei Fu had learned that every herb has a time and a season when its beneficial properties are at their peak and ready for harvest. He also knew that many of the most beneficial herbs could only be grown in extraordinary environments where conditions were near perfect. The humidity. The growing season. The temperature. The altitude. All had to be in perfect balance for many of the rarest, most beneficial herbs to grow.

Exploring the rugged mountains and many of the lush, green valleys of Taiwan was done in the name of collegiate research. Tei Fu, however, found that his love and respect for nature grew with each field trip that he and Oi-Lin shared together. Tei Fu had learned from his studies of the traditional Chinese that throughout their history the people and culture of China have been shaped and molded by an abiding respect for nature, and a genuine recognition of and reverence for the powers of creation. Perhaps more than any other major civilization, the Chinese from the beginning made nature the focus of their culture, art, and philosophies of life.

In the historic Chinese view, life was a puzzle. Solutions were found by observing and imitating nature—a model already perfect in its design. Through understanding nature, man had the best opportunity to "live long and live well." Since herbs and vegetables are the natural gifts from Mother Earth, these were the foods the Chinese historically relied upon to promote health. Consequently, through much of world history, China was the leader in both herbology and agriculture. The iron plow, for example, was used by Chinese farmers 2,200 years ago, centuries before the rest of the world.

The most perfect of God's creations was the human body. If man could keep his body and spirit in tune with nature, the body would function as it was designed—to be healthy, happy and reproductive. Chen knew that herbs provided the basis of many modern medicines. Aspirin, for example, contains a chemical that comes from the white willow bark herb. As Chen would repeat hundreds of times in the years to come, one's body needs vitamin C to be healthy. He would point out that you can get vitamin C by eating a tablet or ingest it in its natural form by eating an orange. "Which do you believe is more beneficial for you," he would ask, "an isolated chemical, or a nutrient in its whole-food form?"

While he was often ridiculed by fellow medical students, to Chen the answer seemed very simple. "Why not live with nature rather than try to conquer it?"

During many discussions with Oi-Lin about the traditional versus the modern approaches to health and medicine, Tei Fu shared his hopes and dreams for the future. Perhaps some day he could open his own herb shop, or even a factory where he could manufacture and sell his own herbal products and formulations. He wanted to find a way to combine the benefits of modern scientific advancement with the ancient traditions of being in harmony with nature. He didn't know how or even if it would ever happen, but that was his goal.

Oi-Lin loved to hear Tei Fu talk of his dreams. Perhaps more than any other quality, that was the one Oi-Lin admired most: Tei Fu Chen was a dreamer. He had vision. He devoted much of his life to examination of the past . . . but he could also see a future. Oi-Lin could see the future as well, and in her future she saw a man named Tei Fu Chen.

∽

Oi-Lin's conversion to Chen's way of thinking about the traditional value of herbs was largely an intellectual process. But she couldn't accept his views about the Mormon religion unless she was both intellectually and spiritually converted. That conversion would come in time. But in late 1970, Oi-Lin and Tei Fu faced a more immediate decision.

They had been together as a "couple" for over a year. It was the first romantic relationship that either had had. In many respects, they seemed so different. And yet on the most important things, their values were much the same. Both Tei Fu and Oi-Lin were very independent and did not pay much concern to how their friends or associates felt about their relationship. They cared deeply, however, about what their families would think.

In the early 1970s, relatively few women studied to be medical doctors and fewer still succeeded. A woman like

Oi-Lin was a rare find. She was beautiful as well as an excellent student. She came from a comfortable background and a city that was the economic hub of Asia. Soon she would be a medical doctor and achieve a social standing envied by almost all Chinese.

Oi-Lin faced one of the most important decisions she would ever face. In making it she established a precedent that would become a pattern for the remainder of her journey through life. After weighing all of the issues she felt important, she then followed the feelings of her heart. Oi-Lin and Tei Fu announced to their friends and family their decision to become husband and wife. Before his graduation, on February 27, 1972, Tei Fu and Oi-Lin were married. A new journey awaited. But first it was a time for celebration.

Most newlyweds can look forward to their first years of marriage as a time when they bond as a couple. But Tei Fu and Oi-Lin had only a few months to begin knowing each other as husband and wife until they were forced apart. Separation in fact was to be more the rule than the exception in the first several years of the Chens' marriage. Military service was mandatory for all young men graduating from college. Tei Fu was required to enroll for a two-year tour of duty in the Taiwanese ROTC.

As a pharmacist, Tei Fu was commissioned a medical officer in the Taiwanese Army. He was stationed at the General Air Force Hospital in Taipei, while Oi-Lin continued to live in Kaoshiung, working toward her medical degree.

Army living conditions were Spartan and the food horrible, but Tei Fu considered himself fortunate. The hospital assignment likely would keep him from possible combat duty. As a medical officer, he would work with sick or injured soldiers and write prescriptions. His two-year obligation would also give him the opportunity to continue studying traditional herbal philosophies.

The other love in his life, Oi-Lin, was constantly on his mind. Several times each month they spent weekends together; holidays typically were with Tei Fu's family in Chia Yi.

Oi-Lin was warmly accepted into Tei Fu's family. Papa Chen in fact wished his son was more like his daughter-in-law. After all, she was an excellent student and destined to become a medical doctor. Although both Mama and Papa Chen were pleased that their son had finally graduated from medical school as a pharmacist, it concerned them that Oi-Lin would likely have a higher professional station in life than her husband. If only Tei Fu had been a better student, they reasoned, he too could have been a medical doctor. Their disappointment was never veiled.

Out of deference and appreciation, soldiers treated by Tei Fu referred to him as "Dr. Chen." It was very common in the military for any medical officer to be referred to as "Doctor." Nothing pleased Chen's parents more than when someone would refer to their son as Dr. Chen.

The reference to Tei Fu as "Dr. Chen" was entirely proper in Taiwan, where the protocols are different than in the United States. As a military officer in Taiwan, the honor was totally justified. Later in his life, however, the title "doctor" would become highly controversial and a point of attack used by those attempting to discredit him. It was beyond comprehension that his own parents would be numbered among his most vocal detractors.

While both of Chen's parents were good to Oi-Lin, she was particularly drawn to Tei Fu's mother. In spite of the hard life that Mama Chen had lived, Oi-Lin considered her a very beautiful woman and enjoyed every opportunity to become better acquainted with her mother-in-law. Mama Chen was the "people person" in the family, Oi-Lin surmised. The middle-aged woman was bright, articulate and had a charm all her own. Had she been born at a different time or place, Oi-Lin thought, she too may have been able to pursue a career and perhaps even become a doctor. But now she was in her mid-forties and it was far more likely that such dreams would be pursued through the lives of her children.

One dream that Mama Chen intended to fulfill for both herself and her children was to move to the United States. In Taiwan, the ultimate ambition was to capture the American Dream. In America, it was perceived, even common people could become wealthy. That belief had been drummed into the minds of the Chen children from the time they were infants. America is a rich land. America is the land of the free. Those who were never able to emigrate to America at least could rationalize their relative poverty. Moving to America created not just the opportunity for financial success—it became the expectation.

But Chen's father didn't know how to get to America. To formally apply and follow a normal course meant years of waiting, and even then most applicants would never be allowed to immigrate. It helped if you knew someone in America who could either sponsor or help you gain admission to an American university. But Papa Chen knew no one in America. However, he did know people in Brazil. He also believed that he had to flee Taiwan.

Taiwan was in the process of being expelled from the United Nations and many in the country feared political upheaval. The prospect that Communist China might take over Taiwan by force was of great concern. With his wife's active encouragement, Papa Chen made a decision that was quite out of character for a former government worker: He sold most of his property and moved with his wife and daughters to Brazil.

No one in the family understood a word of Portuguese, and other than the few acquaintances that Papa Chen had in Brazil, relatively few people there spoke Mandarin Chinese. Chen's father did not seem overly concerned about the language barrier. He had built a reasonably successful life in Taiwan and he saw no reason why he couldn't do the same in Brazil. It would be nearly two years before Tei Fu Chen would see his family again.

In 1974, as Tei Fu's discharge date from the military approached, he and Oi-Lin were faced with difficult decisions. Despite political uncertainty, if they chose to stay in Taiwan, a good and successful life seemed certain. Oi-Lin would soon be graduating from medical school and could open a lucrative medical practice. Tei Fu was qualified to be licensed as a pharmacist, a profession in which he could make a comfortable living. A promising future and high quality of life beckoned them to stay.

But neither Tei Fu nor Oi-Lin had ever been inclined to take the easy route, even for comfort and security. Tei Fu was the dreamer, but both he and Oi-Lin were adventurers. Both also believed that they had a mission—a purpose to their life—and that their destiny would be realized in America.

A second factor would prove decisive in their decision to go to America: Oi-Lin was pregnant. After much consideration, meditation, and prayer, Oi-Lin and Tei Fu came to the same conclusion. If not for themselves, then for their soon-to-arrive daughter and other children who surely would follow, they wanted to become Americans. Children born on American soil are by right U.S. citizens.

While in Brazil, Chen's three sisters there met the Mormon missionaries and all three joined the LDS faith. His older sister, Sheue Wen, had previously joined the LDS Church in Taiwan. Jau-Fang was given the opportunity to study at Ricks College, an LDS-run school in Idaho. She moved from Brazil to Rexburg, a small Mormon community with a population of about 20,000 people, about a four-hour drive from Salt Lake City. Jau-Fang offered to help her brother and his wife gain admission to Ricks' sister institution, Brigham Young University in Provo, Utah. The simplest way to immigrate to America is by enrolling in school. Although Tei Fu had never been particularly enthused about being a student, he had enjoyed college and was confident that the American university system would be much better than Taiwan's.

Oi-Lin was told she could enroll at the University of Utah's medical school. Her studies were scheduled to begin after her daughter's birth. Tei Fu was unable to join her for several months, but Oi-Lin wanted to be certain that her baby would be born in America. In the heat of August and seven-months pregnant, Oi-Lin left Taiwan for Utah. Tei Fu planned to join her four months later after completing his military obligations.

While Oi-Lin was unhappy about the prospect of giving birth to their first child alone, it weighed much heavier on her husband's heart. During Tei Fu's stint in the military, Oi-Lin had become resigned to living apart from her husband. From the time he learned that Oi-Lin was pregnant, Tei Fu was thrilled at the prospect of parenthood. It made no difference whether his firstborn would be a son or a daughter, but it did cause him great distress that he would not be present at the birth.

⮞

Oi-Lin looked forward to being a mother more than any other goal or objective in her life. Her Chinese society may extend great honor to her accomplishment as a medical doctor, but Oi-Lin felt that the greatest honor she could bring to her parents was becoming a parent herself. Because of her mother's lifelong illness, Oi-Lin had had much of the responsibility of nurturing and raising her brothers and sister. She enjoyed family life. Her fondest memories were of family activities. Now she looked forward to children and a family of her own.

Her pregnancy motivated Oi-Lin to do a great deal of introspection and to focus upon some of her most deeply held beliefs. She considered herself a spiritual person. Many times in her life, her heart told her things that her mind simply couldn't understand. She trusted the promptings of her inner voice, and as she contemplated the future of her child, the issue of religion became foremost in her thoughts. Through her husband she had learned a great deal about the Church of Jesus Christ of Latter-day Saints. She appreciated the goodness and simplicity of the LDS faith. She admired the church's standards and family values. Throughout her life, Oi-Lin had been a very diligent and faithful person—as a student, a daughter, and as a wife. The first principle of the Mormon church is *faith*. A promise is given to all those who exercise faith in their study of the gospel of Jesus Christ that they will recognize the truth. Oi-Lin resolved to put her faith to the test and within a short time she felt prompted to convert to the LDS religion. Her mind told her that it would be best for the baby growing within her to be raised in a family that shared a common religion. Her heart told her that the principles of the LDS faith were true.

Tei Fu in elementary school—10 years old, 1958.

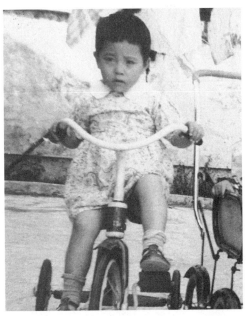

Oi-Lin—2-1/2 years old in front of her
home, 1953.

Tei Fu with his parents and sisters—Jau-Fei, Jau-Hwa, Jau-Fang, and Sheue Wen, 1964.

Oi-Lin preparing to sail to Taiwan to attend medical college—with her father, great aunt, aunt, and cousin, David.

Tei Fu gulping a lunch of rice and
fish cake—a college freshman, 1966.

Tei Fu Chen, the diligent college
student, 1968.

Always a natural speaker, Tei Fu
giving a talk at an LDS meeting
in Kaoshiung.

Tei Fu with fellow officers in the Taipei Air Force during ROTC.

Tei Fu and Oi-Lin, with classmates, doing herbal research, 1969.

Judo competition held at Kaoshiung Medical College—Tei Fu won second place.

The beginning of a lifelong partnership. Tei Fu and Oi-Lin Chen—first formal picture taken as a couple, 1970.

Tei Fu's graduation party in Kaoshiung, Taiwan.

The happy couple at Tai Chung Sun Moon Lake—Oi-Lin wearing a costume of the locals, 1973.

Tei Fu and Oi-Lin on an herbal
research field trip, 1970.

Tei Fu and Oi-Lin at Kaoshiung
Airport, 1973.

Oi-Lin visiting Tei Fu during his ROTC training at
Cheng-Kung Liug, 1972.

Wedding picture in
Tei Fu's hometown of
Chia Yi, 1972.

Custom dictates that the bride be protected from evil with a
traditional bamboo shield.

Tei Fu Chen and class-
mates having a good
time on their college
graduation trip, 1972.

The Chens greet
guests at wedding
celebration.

Tei Fu Chen posing for
the camera in Chia Yi
Park, 1971.

A young Tei Fu in Taiwan with his bicycle—his only means of transportation.

Born to be wild, Tei Fu Chen with his first Yamaha 100cc motorcycle, 1968.

Oi-Lin Chen in anatomy class at Kaoshiung Medical College—she couldn't eat meat for two weeks afterwards, 1971.

Tei Fu gathering herbs while a student in medical college.

Tei Fu and Oi-Lin in the lab at a party with fellow pharmacy students.

Enjoying life in Kaoshiung—a few months before Wendy was born, 1974.

Tei Fu graduating from
Kaoshiung Medical
College, Taiwan, 1972.
Oi-Lin would graduate
three years later. (She
borrowed the cap
and gown.)

Tei Fu graduating in
pharmacy from
Kaoshiung Medical
College, 1972.

Tei Fu and Oi-Lin
celebrating his graduation
with professors.

Oi-Lin Chen working in a biochemistry lab.

Oi-Lin Chen graduating from Kaoshiung Medical College—pictured with the Dean and classmate, 1975.

Oi-Lin gives her judo instructor, Tei Fu, a toss.

CHAPTER SEVEN

Journey
to
America

Flying halfway around the world is a long, tedious journey. For a woman seven and a half months pregnant and traveling alone, the trip from Taiwan to Salt Lake City seemed especially arduous. On the other side of the world, however, a new life and a new country awaited. With that in mind, Oi-Lin looked forward to the trip with trepidation and a spirit of adventure.

With approval of her doctor, Oi-Lin said good-bye to her husband in August 1974, hoping he would join her in Utah once she was able to enroll him as a student at Brigham Young University. Oi-Lin had a visitor's visa and had all the necessary paperwork to travel to the United States.

The flight was indeed long and uncomfortable. Oi-Lin looked forward to seeing her sister-in-law Jau Fang upon her arrival. Chen's sister, however, was unable to make the trip from Idaho where she was a student at Ricks College, and had arranged for a friend to meet Oi-Lin—a friend she had never met—and they traveled the forty miles from Salt Lake City to Provo. Having no place to stay, she checked into the Hotel Roberts, an old decaying structure in downtown Provo where she could rent a room inexpensively.

The next day, Oi-Lin was at BYU. She met a group of Asian students as well as a missionary from Taiwan who knew her husband. He drove her around Provo, stopping first at a local hospital where Oi-Lin was referred to the newest doctor in town. Then they returned to BYU and searched the bulletin board, with Oi-Lin finding a room in someone's house for rent. The last stop was at the admissions office where she enrolled Tei Fu for the winter semester. Her English was not very good and she was a stranger in a strange land, but Oi-Lin had accomplished a great deal her first day in America.

The trim, expansive BYU campus impressed her. With over 25,000 full-time students, the campus was large, clean, green, and beautiful. Provo, on the other hand, seemed small, quaint, and quiet. Unlike Hong Kong and Kaoshiung, there was little traffic, scant noise from the street, and by nine o'clock at night there was hardly a person to be seen. At the intersection where Provo and the BYU campus met were two large signs which carried a challenge for BYU students. The first sign said, "The world is our campus." The second said, "Enter to learn—go forth to serve." Both mottoes pleased the impressionable Oi-Lin.

Nearly two months after she arrived in America, Oi-Lin gave birth to their first child, a daughter she named Wendy. She longed to have her husband or another family member there to rejoice with her at the birth of the eight-pound, four-ounce infant, but only her landlord's wife was at her bedside. Oi-Lin had grown used to being separated from her husband, but on this occasion she felt especially lonely and in need of his support. Nevertheless, with a beautiful, healthy infant in her arms, Oi-Lin had accomplished one of her lifelong dreams—she was now a mother.

Tei Fu would join his wife in three weeks, but his journey to America proved circuitous and difficult. His wife was in America and his parents and sisters were in Brazil. Because he had not yet been admitted to BYU he was unable to get the necessary paperwork to travel from

Taiwan to America. Tei Fu believed the easiest way would be to travel first to Brazil. However, he did not have a visa and Taiwan did not have diplomatic relations with Brazil at the time, so there was no way to go directly to Brazil. Instead, Tei Fu boarded a plane from Taiwan to Paraguay in the belief that it may be easiest to enter neighboring Brazil through Paraguay. Upon arrival in Paraguay he traveled to the border with Brazil. As he approached the checkpoint, however, security guards were closely examining the paper-work of everyone attempting to enter Brazil. Tei Fu almost panicked. He had no passport and no paperwork allowing him to enter Brazil. Fleetingly he considered turning back, but then a strange sense of peace and calm came over him. He approached the border guards prepared to tell them of his plight. The security guards, however, did not ask him a single question nor even to see his documents. They simply waved him through and, suitcase in hand, Tei Fu walked into Brazil. He felt sure that God was with him that day, and was freshly confident he would be able to continue on a month later to join his wife and new daughter in America.

In Brazil, Tei Fu's father, now in his late forties, had made enough money to live comfortably. Mama and Papa Chen had a nice house in Saõ Paulo and had attempted a number of jobs, including the manufacture and sale of plastic plants. His sisters were excited to see him and, knowing of his fascination with herbs, told him of a Chinese doctor who had a rare book containing many herbal formulations. Tei Fu examined the manuscript. Although there was nothing in the book he had not read before, he feigned excitement at the discovery to avoid disappointing his family.

While in Brazil, Tei Fu did discover local herbs that he found intriguing. Some of the herbs were ideal for making balms and oils to enhance and revitalize the skin. He also found a local plant called stevia, which does wonders for the skin and is also a highly concentrated natural sweetener. High-quality stevia leaves can be three to four hundred times sweeter than sugar refined from beets or sugar cane. Chen told himself that this was an herb not to be forgotten.

Since his father's plastics business was only marginally successful, Tei Fu tried to convince him to manufacture essential oils that Tei Fu formulated utilizing the local herbs. At first he resisted, but eventually decided to produce an oil which could be used to relieve headaches and body pain.

Papa Chen personally mixed the ingredients at home in a big tank and then packaged the oil into small bottles. Immediately he encountered red tape with local government officials. Although he had received a license to manufacture the oil, he had to have a pharmacist license to sell the essential oil. Eventually, Papa Chen sold the oil to drug stores, which helped the family through difficult times later in Brazil. As with the stevia, Chen knew that at some point in his life the opportunity would come to market the oil in the United States.

After a month in Brazil and approval of his admission to BYU, Tei Fu was anxious to join his wife and infant daughter in the United States. But again, he faced the challenge of exiting Brazil without a visa. He decided his best hope was to return to Paraguay and apply there for a student visa to America. He approached the border between

Brazil and Paraguay with great anxiety. And once again he simply walked straight through the border behind a busload of tourists without being stopped or questioned. With faith and a prayer, he had secured the necessary paperwork and had boarded a plane in Paraguay for Salt Lake City.

It was late November but Tei Fu had no concept of winter. In Brazil and throughout his life in Taiwan he had lived in warm, tropical climates. When his airplane touched down in Salt Lake City, Tei Fu experienced the first snowstorm of his life. Wearing just a short-sleeve shirt, jeans, and a lightweight jacket, and knowing only a few words of English, it was painfully apparent the young Chinese man was out of his element.

Fortunately for Tei Fu, an older gentleman on the plane who happened to be a BYU professor had taken notice of him and asked if he needed help.

"How did you know?" Tei Fu asked. The professor smiled and responded, "I just had a feeling."

He walked Tei Fu through the airport and together they retrieved their baggage. Since the Salt Lake City airport is about an hour-drive to Provo, the fellow offered Tei Fu a ride. Chen readily accepted. Tei Fu shivered in the bitter cold but felt a genuine warmth from the kindly steward who had befriended him.

Twenty years later, Tei Fu told me about a good-hearted man who had seemed prompted to help the young Chinese immigrant. He handed me a package that contained a rare and valuable replica of an emperor's bronze chariot. On my return to Utah, Tei Fu asked that I stop by the professor's house and deliver the gift on his behalf.

Upon meeting the elderly gentleman, I gave him the package and told him it was from Tei Fu Chen. He smiled broadly and said he remembered well the lonely young man on the flight from Paraguay to Salt Lake City who was wearing a short-sleeved shirt in the middle of winter.

∽

In spite of the total culture shock of Utah and the frigid winter weather, Tei Fu was thrilled to be in America. He was reunited with his wife and saw his baby girl for the first time. Their time together, however, was again short-lived. While Oi-Lin had easily enrolled Tei Fu for undergraduate studies at BYU, she herself had been stymied in attempts to enroll in a U.S. medical school. She faced a series of extremely difficult tests and, with her limited knowledge of English, the chance that she could get her license to practice medicine was extremely slim. Oi-Lin also learned that by completing one more year of medical school in Taiwan she could more easily get her license to practice medicine in America. It was decided that it would be best for Oi-Lin to return to Taiwan, complete her medical studies and hospital internship there, and then return to America as soon as possible.

At the end of 1974, Tei Fu and Oi-Lin celebrated a modest Christmas together. Right after the holidays Oi-Lin and Wendy traveled to Brazil. Tei Fu's parents had agreed that they and his sisters would take care of Wendy while Oi-Lin returned to Taiwan. It would be nearly a year before Tei Fu, Oi-Lin, and Wendy would all be together again.

Tei Fu began his studies at BYU in January 1975, and it proved to be one of the most difficult periods of his life. He was at a new university in a strange country and his wife and daughter were in separate corners of the world. He anguished over missing the first year of his daughter's life and missed Oi-Lin terribly. They were about to celebrate their third anniversary, and had spent more time living apart than together. The young couple wrote each other often. Since they could not afford long distance telephone calls, instead they often exchanged ninety-minute audiocassettes to update one another on their lives and to share the tender feelings of their hearts. On rare occasions they would arrange for a telephone call. Though the calls were infrequent and brief, they greatly lifted each other's spirits.

Tei Fu did everything he could to economize and save money for the long distance phone calls. In America, he had discovered and grown accustomed to the greasy flavors of fast food. A hamburger chain called "Dee's" sold a twenty-four-cent ketchup and mustard hamburger, except on Wednesdays when the price was reduced to nineteen cents. To save a few pennies, every Wednesday Chen would buy a dozen hamburgers, refrigerate them, and then allow himself a daily ration of two hamburgers, until they went on sale again the following Wednesday.

School in Taiwan had never been easy for Tei Fu and now he was immersed in a system that was very different, with classes taught in a language he didn't much understand. Secluded in a dormitory, he spent most of his time studying pharmacology and biochemistry. Tei Fu particularly focused on microbiology, the study of bacteria. It would prove to be an important subject for a pharmacist because microbiology teaches the concepts of sanitization and sterilization. Other than studying and teaching judo, there was little for Tei Fu to do. He was still very shy and found it difficult to make new friends. Fortunately, he had the opportunity to be a lab instructor because of the pharmacy degree he received in Taiwan. Time passed more quickly when he was busy, so he would often study twelve to fourteen hours a day.

By year's end, Oi-Lin and Wendy were finally able to return to the United States. Tei Fu's oldest sister, Sheue Wen, who had protected him as a child, had lovingly looked after his daughter. She traveled from Brazil with Wendy and then continued on to North Dakota where she had enrolled in college. Oi-Lin had arranged the year before for their young family to live in the married student BYU housing project called "Wymount Terrace." The units were small, but clean and inexpensive. With cinder block walls and cold linoleum tile floors, the tiny apartment seemed quite barren. It was the tenants' responsibility to furnish and decorate their dorm. The Chens simply could not afford much furniture, so visitors typically had to sit on the floor.

One evening when the Chens were walking home from the Laundromat where they had done their weekly laundry, they noticed an old sofa that had been set out along the curbside as trash. The fabric on the cushions was torn and shredded and the sofa had no legs, but it hardly seemed like refuse to the young couple. Hurriedly, they took their basket of laundry to the apartment and returned to ask the sofa's owners if they could haul it away. Tei Fu lifted the front end and Oi-Lin the back, and they carried the old sofa home, setting it on four cinder blocks and covering the worn fabric with sheets and blankets. It was their first piece of furniture. They were extremely proud of it.

Tei Fu's visa to the United States would soon expire and he sought to extend it by applying to medical schools throughout America. Despite the constant rejection, he still dreamed of becoming a doctor. Through research at the BYU library he found a medical school in Houston, Texas that he believed was very likely to accept him.

Tei Fu, Oi-Lin, and Wendy packed up their Pontiac and began the twenty-hour drive from Provo to Houston. Neither Tei Fu nor Oi-Lin's parents were in a position to extend much financial support, so the young family lived a frugal existence. Midway through the trip they stopped in New Mexico where they found a hotel for nine dollars for the night. They carried an electric fry pan with them to avoid eating out. They used it to prepare instant noodles—their only meal of the day.

The trip to Texas proved a total waste of time. Chen had convinced himself if he traveled to Texas and met with the admissions officer personally, his chances for acceptance might improve. He was mistaken. As soon as the admissions officer realized that Tei Fu had no green card, the interview was over.

On the return trip from Texas, the Chens, desperate for money, stopped in Reno, Nevada where a friend had told them jobs were plentiful. The couple was down to their last hundred dollars. Reno became home for three months, where Tei Fu worked as a changer and a keno writer at a local casino. His strong work ethic and facility with numbers impressed his supervisors. In just a short time he had become recognized as one of the best keno riders in the city, which created the opportunity for him to work in two casinos—eighty hours a week.

Because of his good reputation, he was able to secure a job for his sister, Sheue Wen, to be a keno writer. Oi-Lin managed the transportation between jobs for both of them. She was also busy preparing for her medical exam and taking care of their daughter, Wendy.

The neon lights and gaming environment gave Tei Fu a second dose of culture shock. From the sleepy Victorian streets of Provo, to the carefree and wild partying in Nevada, America seemed a curious place indeed.

By summer's end, Tei Fu had earned enough money to pay for the next semester's tuition at BYU. The family returned to Provo ready for another year of school. Tei Fu took a part-time position as assistant manager for a 7-Eleven store. Oi-Lin had been offered a position as a research associate at BYU conducting vitamin B_1 research on rats. Her work required that she kill and examine hundreds of the little white creatures. Oi-Lin didn't have the heart to euthanize the mice, so Tei Fu would come into the lab and administer the drops of ether. After two and a half years in the research lab, she landed a position as a physician's assistant at the BYU health center. Although Oi-Lin had not yet received her medical license, she functioned as a nurse practitioner, treating colds and infections and administering physical exams.

CHAPTER EIGHT

Dreams
of
Parents

*C*ompleting his studies at BYU in 1977, Tei Fu's long journey as a student finally came to an end. Now he was faced with the decision of choosing a career. He considered becoming a pharmacist until he discovered how extremely low the initial starting pay was—about $3.75 an hour to intern with a licensed pharmacist.

Their second child, Reuben, was born in June 1978. Shortly after his birth, the Chens had a once in a lifetime experience that was totally unanticipated but very special. Typically they would attend their Sunday church services in a ward (the Mormon term for a parish or congregation) that had been organized just for the Asian students at BYU. But they were late to the meeting and missed the chance to bless their newborn son. Their next opportunity would come on the first Sunday of the following month. On that particular Sunday, however, the Chens did something out of the ordinary and opted to attend their Sabbath meetings in their "home ward" which was made up of the area surrounding their neighborhood. It is customary once each month, as part of the services, to give recently born children a priesthood blessing to bestow the powers of health and spiritual guidance into the infant's life. Usually the blessing is pronounced by the child's father. On this Sunday, however, the parents who had brought their babies to the worship services were to be surprised.

Organ music played and set a reverent tone for the congregation as they took their seats. Just as the meeting was set to begin, the room fell silent. A small, gentle, white-haired man entered the chapel. Everyone in the congregation immediately came to their feet and whispered excitedly to one another. It was Spencer W. Kimball, President of the LDS Church. It was the *living prophet!*

As President Kimball slowly walked down the aisle towards the front of the chapel, he stopped just once and shook the hand of a young Chinese man who stood with his wife, his daughter, and a baby son. He looked into Tei Fu's eyes and smiled in an approving way.

Six babies were blessed that day by President Kimball, including his great-grandson and a baby boy named Reuben Chen. During the meeting the elderly prophet who was revered by millions of people throughout the world offered counsel to the parents in attendance. "Love your children," President Kimball admonished. He explained that that did not necessarily mean to always give them their way. Younger children were to be controlled while teenagers were to be encouraged. "Set boundaries," he said. "Establish guidelines. The greatest influence you will ever have on your children is not through the punishment you administer but through the example you set."

Oi-Lin resolved that Sunday to be the kind of parent that President Kimball described. "I still tell my children what to do, even the older ones." Oi-Lin explains. "Of course they have to decide. They must make their choices. If they make a mistake, I will be there to support them. But I will tell them what I think is best. If I didn't love them, I wouldn't let them know."

Through their lives, Tei Fu and Oi-Lin Chen have observed the many differences of how children are raised in

America as compared to the Chinese culture. One day Tei Fu and I were traveling together and discussing the challenges of raising a family. He noted "Americans are more casual with their children. They express their love and affection more often and more openly. But Chinese parents are more disciplined. They provide greater structure and encouragement for their children to achieve."

I asked him which approach he felt was more effective. He thought for a moment and said, "I think I prefer the American way," he said, remembering the day he met President Kimball.

⤳

With the new addition to the family, Tei Fu sought a stable job that could offer him career opportunities. He especially hoped to find a position where he could use his degree in pharmacology along with his in-depth knowledge of herbs.

When career counselors at BYU were not particularly helpful, one day Tei Fu simply opened the yellow pages and looked for the names of local herbal companies. He found two, Nature's Sunshine and Nature's Way. Since Nature's Sunshine was listed first, he drove to its headquarters in nearby Springville, walked in and asked to fill out an application. On the form he noted his background in both herbs and pharmacology, and he was immediately offered a job in their research and development division.

At that time in America, herbs were used primarily as alternatives to traditional and more expensive medicines and were usually distributed through health food stores. Golden seal root, for example, was for sinus problems.

White willow bark was used to treat headaches for those not wanting to use aspirin. The market for herbal products was very narrow and consisted primarily of people who had had some form of herbal remedy passed down from parents and grandparents.

With a good job finally secured, Chen encouraged his parents and younger sisters to move from Brazil to Utah. He rented a duplex in Orem in which he, Oi-Lin, and their two children lived on the main floor while Jau-Fei and Jau-Hwa lived in the basement with their parents. Jau-Fang and Sheue Wen were already both married and did not live with them.

This period gave Chen the first real opportunity to spend time with his younger two sisters and build a relationship. He was eleven years older than Jau-Hwa and fourteen years older than Jau-Fei, so he had never had much opportunity to get to know his sisters in Taiwan. Now that the sisters were approaching adulthood, it was much easier for the family to relate to one another.

As the youngest and most beautiful of the sisters, Jau-Fei continued to be the princess of the family. Although Jau-Hwa was not mistreated, it was Jau-Fei who was the family jewel. She simply could do no wrong.

Years later, Jau-Hwa would confide to one of the early distributor leaders how hurtful it was for her to hear her mother tuck her younger sister into bed, give her a kiss, and tell her that she was the beautiful one night after night. And then walk past Jau-Hwa saying nothing. It would be easy to conclude that this nightly ritual damaged her self-esteem and created a mind-set that to have her mother's approval she must first and foremost look out for her younger sister, Jau-Fei.

When the two sisters were students at BYU, often they would study together at the library after class. Jau-Hwa, who was older and driving the family car, would prepare to leave and ask Jau-Fei if she wanted a ride home. "No thanks. I'll find a way later," Jau-Fei would say. So Jau-Hwa would leave, return to their home, and within fifteen to twenty minutes the telephone invariably would ring and Jau-Fei would inform her mother that she was ready to come home.

"Jau-Hwa, go get your sister right now," the mother would command. And being the obedient daughter she was, Jau-Hwa would turn around, drive back to BYU, and pick up her sister, all without a word of complaint. Jau-Hwa lived in the shadow of Jau-Fei and was at Jau-Fei's beck and call whenever the mother dictated.

It is not uncommon for parents to attempt to live their dreams through their children. In the Chinese culture, the mother's dreams are often lived through the daughter, especially when the mother has lived a hard and meager existence as Mama Chen had. Her dreams had been real and unfulfilled, but it was not too late. She had a bright and beautiful daughter. Jau-Fei was more than willing to be the vehicle for her mother's ambition; for want of a mother's approval, daughters will do almost anything.

From the time she was very young, Jau-Fei proudly played the piano. She was attractive and believed herself to be talented. She enjoyed the attention she received whenever she played. When the Chen family moved from Brazil to the United States, Tei Fu began to look for a small house where the entire family could live. He searched for weeks, but with each prospect he located, his mother would examine the house and reject it because the living room was too small for a baby grand piano.

Several years later, during Sunrider's early success, Tei Fu gave his parents a gift of several thousand dollars. Papa Chen was driving an old beat-up pickup truck at the time, and Chen suggested they use the money to purchase a new car. Instead, Tei Fu's mother wanted a piano.

"But Mom," Tei Fu objected, "if you buy a car, everyone will get to ride in it. If you use the money for a piano, only Jau-Fei can play it."

They purchased the piano.

Jau-Fang was the only one of Chen's sisters with whom he never was able to spend much time. While the family lived in Brazil, Jau-Fang had immigrated to America to attend college. She had met a Caucasian man at Ricks College and married him. Chen's father objected bitterly. He directly confronted Tei Fu, asking him why he had allowed his sister to marry a Caucasian and implying that the choice had been his and not hers. Jau-Fang had also approached her father, asking for a loan to help her husband open a dental clinic. Papa Chen refused and years would pass before father and daughter would speak to one another again.

❧

Although Tei Fu thoroughly enjoyed his job as a researcher for Nature's Sunshine, there was a power struggle brewing in senior management, along with rumors that the owner of the company intended to sell it soon. Chen hoped to find a comparable position at a more stable company. In late 1979, Tei Fu was offered a position as the research director for another Utah herbal company, Nature's Way. Like Nature's Sunshine, it too promoted products derived from American herbs through retail health food stores as well as through a direct sales marketing subsidiary called Natural Life.

~

As the only in-law living among a family of Chens, Oi-Lin worked hard to fit in. She had always enjoyed and gotten along well with her in-laws but difficulty arose after she had her medical degree. She had accomplished what neither her father-in-law nor his son had been able to do. Resentment was accompanied by an implied expectation that whatever Oi-Lin accomplished, Jau-Fei should do better. Disparaging and hurtful comments from Tei Fu's parents, especially the mother, became more frequent.

"The medical school in Taiwan is very weak," Oi-Lin's mother-in-law would say. "It would have been much better had you been able to get your medical degree in the United States."

Whatever Oi-Lin's accomplishments, they were downplayed by Mama Chen. Having never had much of a relationship with her own mother, Oi-Lin very much wanted the respect and approval of her mother-in-law. But she had too much going for her: Oi-Lin had gotten into medical school, was about to establish a medical practice, and was beautiful. She was even a talented pianist.

For most parents, Oi-Lin would have been the ideal daughter-in-law. But instead of embracing Oi-Lin, Mama Chen saw her as a threat to her own daughter, Jau-Fei. Oi-Lin could not be the answer to Mama Chen's unrealized dreams. Jau-Fei was the anointed one.

Bad news came Oi-Lin's way in 1981 when hospitals in Utah refused to recognize her Taiwanese degree. She was required to do a second residency to obtain her medical license in the U.S. She was accepted to join the residency program at the Shadyside Hospital in Pittsburgh, Pennsylvania. Yet another separation loomed. The relationship between Tei Fu and his wife was solid, however, and they had learned to endure nearly every form of hardship. Another year of separation did not seem too great a burden to bear, though it would not be easy on any of the family— which now included three children, Wendy, Reuben and Sunny, who accompanied Oi-Lin to Pennsylvania.

In Pittsburgh, Oi-Lin found a small two-bedroom apartment as well as a nanny/ housekeeper who could stay with the children during her long hours at the hospital. For a thousand dollars a month, Oi-Lin often worked eighty hours a week. She intended eventually to set up a family practice, and so the rotation from OB/GYN to surgery to internal medicine gave her a broad perspective and experience. Witnessing firsthand the pain and suffering and frequently death was difficult for Oi-Lin, especially watching the families in the oncology or cancer care unit. Often by the time the cancer was diagnosed there was simply not much hope or help to be offered.

During the day Oi-Lin made her hospital rounds, and

often in the evening she was assigned to the emergency room which was flowing with blood from shootings and stabbings and traumatized by those with drug overdoses. She saw the hard side of America and American life. Perhaps what disturbed her most, however, were some of the more experienced doctors. Usually with their patients they were outwardly caring and interested in their well-being. However, once the patients were under anesthesia, these same doctors became rude, insensitive, mocking, and sometimes quite careless. Oi-Lin made a silent commitment to herself that her character would be the same whether the patient was awake or asleep.

As difficult as these times were for Oi-Lin, she also knew how hard they must have been on her three children. She and Wendy, Reuben, and Sunny slept in one bedroom with the housekeeper in another. Many nights Oi-Lin was at work and simply had no sleep at all. Patients often died at night, and in the course of a death or an emergency, Oi-Lin didn't feel she could leave when her shift was over even though she was free to do so. On weekends she would take her children to a playground. While they ran through the park and played on the swing sets, she would sit on a park bench and struggle to stay awake.

Unlike when she was fulfilling her residency in Taiwan and felt a total separation from her husband, at least now he would phone regularly and occasionally find an inexpensive airfare and fly back to Pittsburgh for a brief visit. As a result of one such visit, six months into her residency Oi-Lin found that she was once again pregnant.

She was now a pregnant "single mom" in a tough

city working eighty hours a week and trying to rear three children. But although Oi-Lin couldn't explain it, in her own way she felt good about both her circumstances and her life. Within months she would be a licensed medical doctor. She had a loving and supportive husband and three beautiful children with a fourth one on the way. While not her expectation of the American Dream, her life was full and happy. In July 1982 with her residency finally complete, Oi-Lin returned to Provo and soon received her medical license.

It was time for Tei Fu and Oi-Lin to live on their own as a family. They bought a large six-bedroom house in Orem, Utah for about $140,000. That was a lot of money in 1982, but with Tei Fu's job as a research and development director at Nature's Way, and now that Oi-Lin was a licensed physician, they felt confident they could handle the mortgage payments. "Besides," Oi-Lin pointed out, "I can use the basement of our home to establish my medical practice." Eric, their fourth child, was born on October 10, and Oi-Lin liked the flexibility afforded by having her medical practice in her home. She specialized in internal medicine and throughout the day was also able to shuttle the kids to school and on to piano and violin lessons.

Many people, including other physicians and pharmacists, told Oi-Lin that the only way she could succeed as a medical doctor was to open up a "real office," to advertise and actively solicit referrals, and to grow her practice to where she could see dozens of patients every day. Oi-Lin responded by simply saying that that was "not my nature." Most physicians worked to make money. Oi-Lin worked because being a medical doctor was her profession, her life-long dream, and a calling that gave her a great deal of fulfillment. Once a week she treated patients at a nursing home. Because of their advanced ages, many of the patients were quite ill and it was not uncommon to see them move from the nursing home to the hospital to the mortuary. The elderly nursing home residents grew fond of Oi-Lin and looked forward to her visits. They appreciated her caring and sensitive nature and also looked forward to the occasions when she brought along her newborn son to show off.

Female doctors were not common in America in the early 1980s and were especially rare in Orem, Utah. Visiting a female Chinese doctor in a community that is almost entirely Caucasian was an adventure for some and too far "out of the box" for others. Her patients, however, invariably were impressed with her and word-of-mouth referrals generated more business than Oi-Lin felt capable of handling.

It was a real family affair at the Chen home, where Oi-Lin's patients could hear the kids upstairs practicing the piano, and occasionally Wendy or Reuben would help register patients upon their arrival. But what impressed the locals was Oi-Lin's thoroughness and the time and attention she devoted to each patient. She respected her clients and rarely kept anyone waiting for their appointment. Her practice was a bit of an oddity in the Provo/Orem medical community, but one that numerous people came to appreciate.

CHAPTER NINE

East
Meets
West

If a Chinese female doctor seemed a bit of an oddity in Orem, Utah, so did a Chinese herbalist at Nature's Way. The Nature's Way approach to herbs was strictly "American." Most products were based upon formulas by Dr. John R. Christopher, a colorful and charismatic individual who seemed larger than life. He was a portly fellow with a twinkle in his eye, wavy white hair, and a meticulously trimmed mustache. In his black double-breasted pinstripe suit, Christopher became the chief promoter and spokesman for Nature's Way. Crisscrossing the country lecturing on the benefits of herbs, he talked about his own cancer and the role of herbs in providing natural solutions to medical problems, as well as the power of herbs as substitutes for drugs. Most of Nature's Way products were herbs like echinacea, milk thistle, valerian root, and bee pollen.

Tei Fu spent most of his time working with Nature's Way's small multi-level marketing division, called Natural Life, which had paltry sales of about $150,000 a month.

Twenty years ago, the concept of multi-level or network marketing wasn't nearly as widespread as it is today. Network marketing companies sell their products to independent distributors who make money by selling them to their "personal groups" and through recruiting additional distributors who sell products to their networks of friends and families. Distributors earn commissions on the volume of products they sell as well as upon what the other distributors in their "networks" sell.

Amway, founded in 1959, is now and was then the

largest multi-level marketing company in the world. Just as
Utah was to become well known for the many herbal nutritional companies based there during the 1980s and 1990s,
literally hundreds of network marketing companies would
also have their origins in Utah, a traditionally industrious
state whose symbol is, appropriately, the beehive.

The president of Natural Life was a young man in his
mid-thirties named Dean Black. A former BYU professor
who had taught physiology, Dean had been attracted to the
business world in the hope that he could generate a better
income to support his large and growing family.

Dr. Black was impressed with the young Chinese
herbalist from the time of their first introduction at a Natural Life staff meeting. Tei Fu made a much deeper impression a short time later when Dean complained to him about
his chronic suffering from hay fever allergies.

"I was handed a plastic bag of this horrible-looking
green powder and Chen told me to take a teaspoon of it
before every meal," recalls Black. "Within two weeks I was
absolutely symptom free. I was astounded. I became very
excited about the possibilities and asked Tei Fu what the
herb was that he had given me."

Chen explained that it wasn't a single herb but a formulation of many herbs. The recipe was based upon Chinese philosophies and experience developed through many
generations of time. With that introduction, Tei Fu began
sharing with Black the traditional Chinese approaches
towards herbs and health. What Black learned was substantially different from the way that Natural Life was promoting Dr. Christopher's products.

The most significant difference, Chen explained, was that the Chinese have traditionally believed that the greatest value of herbs was to promote and maintain health rather than treat illness or disease. Christopher's approach instead was typical of modern western civilization: When there is a problem with your body or one of its systems, take a pill or a medicine or an herb to remedy the problem. Chen characterized the American approach as "substitution." Wasn't it better, he reasoned with Black, to use herbs to promote and maintain wellness rather than treat disease?

To achieve optimum health the Chinese believed the body must be "in balance." This could be best achieved through the principles of Yin and Yang. Some herbs promote the "Yin" function by putting into the body the proper and necessary nutrients to nourish each of the body's vital systems. Other herbs are Yang herbs which facilitate the "out" function, cleansing the body's systems of the wastes, pollutants and toxins to which people are exposed or may ingest. The concept of Yin and Yang as it relates to health seemed quite simple: Through utilizing a variety of herbs to nourish and to cleanse, the body can reach its own healthy state of balance.

A more complicated traditional Chinese philosophy in which Chen firmly believed was called the "Circle of the Quinary." All of nature is composed of five basic elements—metal, wood, water, fire, and earth. Nature is in harmony when each of the five elements works in concert with the other. Just as there are five elements, the Chinese believed there were five basic systems of the body, each of which has the character of nature's five elements. The circulatory system is represented by water; the immune system by wood; the endocrine or reproductive system by fire; the digestive system by earth; the respiratory system by metal. Just as in nature, optimum health can only exist when each of the body's five systems is working in harmony with the others. Tei Fu used simple analogies to make his point. A chariot may be pulled by five strong and healthy horses, but unless the horses function collectively as a team, chaos can result. Harmony among the five is just as important as individual strength in achieving the desired result. Another simple example that Chen used to illustrate the body's five systems was to compare the body to a house. A builder, noted Chen, could use the very finest building materials but the materials or ingredients alone would not determine the quality of the house. If the house had five rooms it would be the design of the house and how the five rooms related to one another that would ultimately determine how functional the home would be.

The point that Chen hoped to make was that to achieve overall health it was necessary to do more than simply nourish and cleanse each of the body's five systems. The means by which the five systems were connected and related to one another was a vital consideration in herbal formulations.

The more Dean Black was educated in the Chinese concepts of health and nutrition, the more convinced he became that Natural Life needed to develop an herbal product line that embraced the Chinese philosophies. He encouraged Tei Fu to develop a "Dr. Chen" line of five herbal products designed to address the needs of the five body systems.

Recalls Black: "I figured that Nature's Way could be the Dr. Christopher line of herbs and Dr. Chen could do the Natural Life line." Dean Black realized that the Chinese philosophies were far more sophisticated than what Christopher and Nature's Way were presently promoting. Black concluded that the Natural Life network marketing distributors ideally could be trained to teach the concepts and the romance of the Chinese philosophies to generate customer interest. It was clear that health food store retailers were resistant to the idea of Chinese products because no one had ever taught them the basic concepts of Chinese herbs and herbal formulations.

Black was also aware that Natural Life distributors were discouraged that the same products they were attempting to market through direct sales were offered in many health food stores. Most consumers simply chose the convenience of stopping by a retail store rather than contacting a Natural Life distributor.

Dean Black and Tei Fu Chen together approached Ken Murdock, owner of Nature's Way, with the idea of launching Dr. Chen's line of Chinese herbs. Murdock listened carefully and then reached a very quick conclusion. "America is not ready for Chinese herbs," Murdock said matter-of-factly, sending Tei Fu back into the lab to work on the American herbal product formulations. Black persisted, however. He begged Murdock at least to let them give it a try. An herbs and natural foods convention was being held in Las Vegas, and Murdock consented to a Nature's Way booth which featured a life-size cutout of Tei Fu Chen along with free samples of the Chinese product line. The test marketing was a colossal failure. On the surface, customers had no interest in Chinese herbs, and without a detailed explanation of how the products worked, interest could not be generated. The Chinese products and philosophies were new and substantially different and retail customers simply would not take the time to explore the new possibilities.

Chen and Black both felt, however, that through network marketing potential customers could be taught enough about the Chinese philosophies that they would at least be willing to give the products a try. But Murdock was dead set against it.

One Natural Life distributor named Don Caster also owned three retail health food stores in Ohio called The Raisin Rack. He sold Nature's Way's products through traditional network marketing and also stocked them in his stores. Caster also believed that in the 1970s America was not yet ready for Chinese herbs. "The herbal market then was strictly an alternative to medicine," Caster explained. "Most people didn't even talk about herbs openly in public." The American experience with things Chinese was very limited. At that time, China was a closed communist country. It had only been a few years since President Nixon had traveled to China to begin opening relations between the two countries.

"So the idea that the Chinese might have a better approach towards food and health than the Americans was difficult for most of us to accept," said Caster. "We weren't ready for Chinese herbs then because we didn't know any better. The Chinese philosophy was totally foreign to the mainstream view of herbs and health."

For the few Chinese products that Ken Murdock did allow Chen to develop in the research and development lab, it was necessary for Chen to locate suppliers for the Chinese herbs. Since Chen was the only one in the company who could speak Chinese, Murdock allowed him to start a small import company, called TF Chen Products, to import the herbs from China. Chen would then sell the herbs to Nature's Way with a very minimal markup.

To get money to start the business, Chen went first to his father and asked for a loan of $40,000. His father immediately refused, saying that Tei Fu already had a good job and that attempting to engage in an entrepreneurial exercise on the side was foolhardy.

"You're just a Chinese boy and you want to compete with Americans in America!" he said mockingly. "You have no chance. You will fail."

For the most part, Tei Fu understood why his father was so negative. Tei Fu had poor English skills and most small businesses do in fact fail; the odds seemed stacked against him. Chen's father had never enjoyed much success in his own business enterprises and found it difficult to believe that his son could succeed where the father had not.

Tei Fu sensed that it was not just an issue of whether he could succeed. To his father it was also a matter of face. He didn't *want* his son to succeed in the business world. He wanted him to do the responsible thing, just as he had done: Work a good, steady job, avoid unnecessary risks, and be the obedient son.

The house in which Tei Fu's parents lived was in both the father and the son's name, so Chen asked his father whether he could use the home as collateral to obtain a loan from the bank.

"Don't be foolish," his father replied. "You have a good job. Don't put your future at risk. If you want to wipe out your life savings, I can't stop you. But I won't allow you to destroy mine." The next day Papa Chen demanded that Tei Fu sign a paper removing his name from the deed of trust on their home. Tei Fu felt discouraged and deflated. Oi-Lin consoled him by offering to call her father to see whether he would be willing to lend Tei Fu the money necessary for him to start his import business. Oi-Lin's father immediately agreed and in 1981 TF Chen Products was in business.

Chen continued to work as director of research and development for Nature's Way. But he was extremely frustrated. Most herbal companies back then simply ground up herbs and put them in capsules, identifying which herb was most beneficial in treating which disease. Chen could not understand why Murdock failed to see the potential of a product line of Chinese herbal formulations based upon the Philosophy of Regeneration with five formulations designed for each of the five major body systems. Instead of using herbs as a substitute for drugs or as a cure-all, why not use herbs to help the body be nourished and cleansed and strengthened in a natural way? Dean Black was convinced and continued to lobby Murdock. Finally Murdock agreed to produce a small Chinese product line. But the sales were disappointing and Murdock lost interest.

But Chen could not let his dream die. Just as Oi-Lin's medical practice began to blossom and their family finally began enjoying a degree of normalcy and stability, Tei Fu

told Oi-Lin that it was important that they once again carefully reconsider their future. After two and a half years at
Nature's Way, he was considering quitting his job. He
didn't want to do it unless Oi-Lin felt the same degree of
confidence about his future plan as he did.

Tei Fu was at one of the most critical crossroads of his
life. He had a dream, a vision that he felt in his heart could
be achieved. He knew he could make better, more effective
products than what Natural Life was willing to offer. He
knew there was great potential in multi-level marketing. It
did not seem far-fetched that people could gather groups of
other people together to talk about Chen's products and
the traditional Chinese philosophies. He knew that he
could motivate distributors with both his products and with
the opportunity to make money and achieve financial independence. The concept of network marketing is one in
which Chen wholeheartedly believed. He felt it was the best
way to do business because it is the fairest way of rewarding
those who work hard and achieve results, and for many
people it may be their one opportunity to achieve prosperity. Most people never have the opportunity to go into
business because of the high demands of up-front money
and capital investment. But in multi-level marketing, all
people need is a desire to work and an enthusiasm for the
product. Chen often thought back to his early days in
Provo, when he and Oi-Lin so desperately needed additional income. He realized that providing a means for
people to generate additional family income could have as
beneficial impact on their lives as would his herbal products
which promoted health.

What Chen envisioned had never been done before. But after great deliberation and much discussion with Oi-Lin and Dean Black, in 1982 Tei Fu Chen decided to pursue his dream and follow his heart. Yes, it would be against all odds. And yes it was possible that he would fail. But he had read a quote from an American president, Theodore Roosevelt, which inspired him onward: "Far better it is to dare mighty things, to win glorious triumphs even though checked with failure, than to take rank with those poor spirits who neither suffer much nor enjoy much because they live in that gray twilight that knows neither victory nor defeat."

With mixed feelings, Tei Fu and Dean Black walked into Ken Murdock's office and handed him their resignations. They told him of their plans to start a competing firm but promised they would conduct themselves in an ethical manner and would not attempt to take any of his distributors. Murdock made an intriguing counter-offer. Would they consider buying the Natural Life subsidiary for $250,000? Murdock pointed out that it would give them an instant distribution network and would relieve him of the headaches of having retail and multi-level marketing competitors. Further, Murdock offered that the $250,000 could be paid over a five-year payment plan at $50,000 a year, with the first payment not due until the end of the first year of business. It was an offer Chen felt he could not refuse—especially since his existing employment contract stated that he could not work for a competing herbal company for two years after leaving Murdock.

Chen considered going again to his father to ask for a

loan, but because Papa Chen had been so adamant in his previous rejection, Chen decided to simply take the gamble and hope that he would be able to deliver a check for $50,000 to Murdock at the end of his first year.

In December 1982, Tei Fu Chen and Dean Black formed their new company. With the restrictions of Nature's Way no longer an obstacle, Tei Fu resolved that he would do business in his own way which would be unique to his company. Instead of simply grinding up individual herbs, he intended to offer highly concentrated herbs formulated in exacting combinations to be eaten daily as part of a healthy diet. All of his formulations would be built upon the Philosophy of Regeneration rather than substitution. Chen intended to process his herbs in a way that maintained their synergy as a whole food rather than as a chemical isolate. He made one other commitment: Regardless of the herbal formulation or product that he manufactured, he would make it so unique and so superior that in a very real sense he would have no competition.

Chen looked forward to continuing to work with Dean Black, in part because he had been so helpful at Natural Life, and as a Chinese man with poor English skills, Chen needed a strong American counterpart.

Dean Black was articulate and an excellent writer. He too was a philosopher, and their company was all about introducing a new philosophy, a new way of thinking to the American public. Dean assumed responsibility for organizing, translating, and communicating the Chinese mind-set into English.

Before Chen was prepared formally to open the doors

of his business, he and Dean embarked upon a ten-hour drive from Provo to Lake Tahoe, Nevada to meet with the graphic designer who had agreed to create a logo for Chen's company as payment for herbs that Chen had given the artist during the previous several years. Before designing a logo, however, it was obviously necessary for Tei Fu to come up with a name for his new company. He had hoped that at some point during the long drive to Tahoe an idea would come to mind.

During the entire ten-hour trip, however, despite considerable discussion over name possibilities, neither Dean nor Tei Fu had any ideas that both felt comfortable with. By the time they reached the designer's office they still didn't have an idea, so they turned around and drove ten hours back home. The return trip was no more fruitful, and when Tei Fu dropped Black off at his house, they both felt that they had wasted two days. As Tei Fu was returning to his home, discouraged, the sun was setting. He walked in the door and found a room where he could sit quietly and ponder. He felt a sense of inspiration. He ran to the phone and hurriedly called Dean Black.

"I just had an idea come to my mind—a vision of riding the sun," he blurted out enthusiastically to Black. "If you ride the sun, the day never ends. That's our name—Sunrider!"

The more Chen thought about the name "Sunrider," the more excited he became. Since sunlight is the source of all life on earth, reasoned Chen, there were many possibilities and implications. Herbs grow as a result of the sun, and humankind can benefit from the plants offered by nature.

The sun is the primary source of light and direction for all living things. Sunrider could embrace all people who appreciate the power of nature, who are enriched by the sun, and who are lovers of life. Yes, that was it—Sunrider!

CHAPTER TEN

Walk
with
Destiny

After only one month in business, Sunrider published its first *SunWriter* magazine. It was actually just a four-page, one-fold newspaper that featured on its cover some of Sunrider's first distributors, including Ruth Van-Buren (now Ruth LaSalle) and Marv Peterson, who was a track coach and dean at Weber State College. Both Ruth and Marv were very health conscious and were attracted to Sunrider's "Total Health Program." Dean Black was the publisher and editor of Sunrider's news magazine, which regularly featured Dr. Chen discussing traditional Chinese philosophies of health.

Sunrider's flagship products were called Nutrien and Calli Tea. Nutrien had been formulated by Chen based on his study of the Chinese manuscripts. While Nutrien was designed to provide the body with basic nutrition, Calli Tea was promoted as a cleansing beverage that could help purify the body of fats, wastes and toxins. Nutrien concentrate and Calli Tea were the basis of what Sunrider termed its "total health program." From its start, Sunrider promoted wellness through proper nutrition rather than a medicinal approach to herbs. Much time was spent promoting Sunrider's "Philosophy of Regeneration" which held that a properly nourished and cleansed body has the innate ability to maintain optimum health and ward off disease.

TruSweet was offered as a natural sweetener, extracted and concentrated from the herb known as stevia. At that time, stevia was widely used in the Far East as well as in South America as both a natural sweetener and an herb that was helpful in the regulation of blood sugar. Additionally, Sunrider offered a variety of other herbs and herbal formulations.

From the beginning, Sunrider products were the basis of the company's success. The positioning of the products seventeen years ago was not much different than it is today. Sunrider products were based upon ancient Chinese philosophies of balance and whole-food nutrition. They were the only herbal products offered that were concentrated rather than simply encapsulated ground herbs. From the outset, Sunrider promoted its formulations as the finest herbal products in the marketplace.

"Concentration Creates Product Excellence" was the headline in the July 1983 *SunWriter* magazine. Tei Fu explained the uniqueness of his products: "In concentrating a plant, we remove the bulk, the non-nutritive parts of the plant; in other words the cellulose and fiber. After the bulk is removed, the nutrients are left—the vitamins, the minerals, fatty acids, proteins, and carbohydrates."

Chen then emphasized the necessity of retaining the nutrients in their natural, original form. "It is very important that we preserve the precise balance of the nutrients in the original plant or we lose most of the benefit. No one else has achieved that. That is what makes our process unique."

Tei Fu Chen and Dean Black also recognized the importance of creating a motivating marketing and compensation plan for multi-level marketing distributors who excelled.

One of those was Marv Peterson of Weber State College. "Back in February of 1983, I was invited to a meeting that Dean Black and Dr. Chen gave in Salt Lake City for a group of health professionals," recalled Peterson. "I had to travel forty miles to Salt Lake City. It was a very snowy night and there weren't a lot of people there. I was, however, very impressed with what they had to say. Especially the Philosophy of Regeneration which they were espousing. I was on the college faculty at Weber State University and had been on campus there for over twenty-five years. I had taught health classes and was very well aware of contemporary health issues. The philosophies that Chen discussed intrigued me, as did the products that he talked about such as Quinary, Nutrien and Calli.

"But I was also very interested in the opportunity to make some extra money. As a teacher and coach, it seemed it was always a struggle to make ends meet. After the meeting I did start buying some products. I was in very good physical condition but immediately noticed that I had more energy and more stamina, and with six children you need lots of extra energy!"

In addition to teaching, coaching, and volunteer church activities, Peterson was also active in local politics, having served a four-year term on the city council. He didn't have much available time but committed to set aside every Saturday to build the Sunrider business. "Every Saturday I met with groups of people to talk about the phenomenal results that I had experienced from the Sunrider products, as well as to explain the income potential. Within two years and on a part-time basis, I was making several thousand dollars from Sunrider each month."

Less than six months after Sunrider was launched, Chen bought a new car—fulfilling one of the dreams he had had as a youth in Taiwan when no one except the very rich drove automobiles. In July 1983 Chen introduced his Auto Fund program. Twelve Sunrider distributors qualified for new cars, purchased by Sunrider. Many of the distributors, including Jim and Ann Cue, Don Caster, Glenda Feilen, Grey and Paul Jensen, and Sharon Farnsworth, are still active Sunrider distributors.

The first Sunrider to actually acquire his car was Spencer Poch, who had become a Sunrider distributor shortly after the company was founded in December of 1982. Poch chose a large, stylish, blue and white customized Chevrolet van. He had the Sunrider logo etched on the large side windows. A picture of a smiling Poch sitting in the driver's seat of his new van was featured in one of the first *SunWriter* magazines.

Within months of the company's creation, Chen embarked upon building a huge warehouse and distribution center which could also serve as company headquarters. Chen's father, Yung-Yeuan, had been put in an awkward position with Sunrider's early success. On one hand, he had discouraged his son from starting Sunrider and had been very vocal in predicting that his son would fail. On the other hand, the excitement and early success of the company made the elder Chen proud.

Tei Fu wanted desperately for his father to support him and be part of Sunrider's success. He looked for every opportunity to involve both his father and his sisters in the company. Because of Papa Chen's background in the field of architectural engineering, where he had overseen many construction projects, Tei Fu asked his dad to oversee the construction of their new warehouse. He featured his father's work in *SunWriter* and paid tribute to his parents and sisters. The *SunWriter* article read: "As construction progressed, it became evident that one individual was responsible for this project's 'trueness'—Yung-Yeuan Chen, who is the father of Tei Fu Chen." The article continued, "He [Papa Chen] and his wife, Huang Lan Chen, have five children. Many Sunriders have met Dr. Chen and his younger sister, Jau-Hwa. It is easy to see that the building concepts of straight and true have been used in rearing children also." The article concluded, "What good is there in building great structures, if you fail to build the man. That sentiment certainly is born out in the life of Yung-Yeuan Chen."

Just one year after Sunrider had begun operation, Tei Fu and Dean Black reflected on the company's early dramatic success. It began in a small 1,500 square-foot office space. That space had increased to a total area exceeding 27,000 square feet within the year. Sunrider had started with just Dean Black, Tei Fu, and three employees. By year's end their staff had grown to over thirty people. Sales volume expanded ten to twenty percent *each month* over the first year. In December 1983, after just one year, Sunrider's sales volume had grown to $330,000. The staff celebrated their first anniversary with cake, and decorated Tei Fu's office with bouquets of balloons. "It was one of the happiest days of my life!" Tei Fu recalls.

Chen attributed the company's early success primarily

to two factors. First, he said to his distributors, "Product strength is the basis for much of the rapid growth that has taken place. A full line of herbal concentrates supports the Total Health Program of Nutrien Concentrate, Calli Tea and TruSweet." Second, Chen credited Sunrider's pioneer distributors for the company's success: "And speaking frankly, that is the most promising aspect in the Sunrider growth pattern. A handful of faithful distributors have been joined by thousands of Sunriders throughout the country. Our latest mailing will reach 8,000 of you great Sunrider folks."

A few months later, Sunrider hosted in Provo, Utah its second convention for distributors from throughout the United States and Canada. From Alaska to New Jersey, from California to Texas to Canada, hundreds of new Sunrider distributors flocked to Provo to learn more about the company and to be taught by Tei Fu Chen.

Although on a smaller scale, the convention then was very much like the annual conventions Sunrider holds today. New products were introduced. New marketing literature and training programs were unveiled. Sunrider's top distributors were honored in award ceremonies. A variety show was held following dinner, in which Sunrider distributors were asked to display their talents for their fellow Sunriders at the convention. Some sang. Some danced. The evening was capped by a kung-fu and karate demonstration by Dr. Chen. A beautiful piano performance by a little eight-year-old girl named Wendy Chen concluded the evening, and the entire event earned a well-deserved standing ovation.

During one convention session, Chen was answering questions from the audience. One distributor asked if he had been surprised by Sunrider's stunning growth and success during its first year of operation. Chen thought for a moment and then gave a heartfelt response:

> No, I am not so much surprised as I am *relieved*. For over ten years I have had a dream that I would have a company such as Sunrider. I believed we could offer the world the precious philosophies of health that were developed by the traditional Chinese—a company where I could offer people the finest whole-food herbal concentrates in the world. More than just a dream, I have always felt that this was my *destiny*. Living my dream is a wonderful experience. I hope that through Sunrider, thousands of others can also live their dreams of health and prosperity.
>
> I am not surprised. Starting your own company, especially when you're a young Chinese in a foreign land, is a frightening thing to do. Many discouraged me from starting. There were many obstacles to overcome. But when you feel something is right, when you know it in your heart, you do whatever has to be done. Sunrider has a mission and a purpose, just as you and I have a destiny and a purpose. How we fulfill our purpose we may not always know. But whether we choose to follow our dreams is something that each of us can decide.

The enthusiasm and spirit of camaraderie that was felt for three days in February 1984 in Utah was to become contagious. Tei Fu believed Sunrider was on the edge of a frontier of great success. But even in his wildest dreams, he could not envision the broad dimensions of the international success which were about to come Sunrider's way.

Throughout the decade of the eighties, Sunrider would grow faster than even the most successful companies in the world. Along with its success, Sunrider would face stiff challenges and obstacles, none of which were a part of Chen's youthful dreams. Chen's walk with destiny would prove to be largely an uphill journey.

CHAPTER ELEVEN

Clouds
on the
Horizon

Summers in Provo, Utah are usually accompanied by sunny skies. In the warmth of June 1984, Sunrider distributors from throughout the United States and Canada had once again gathered in Utah for a three-day convention. The theme was meant to share Chen's vision, "Ride the Sun." During the convention, Chen was notified by the Utah State Department of Agriculture that the sale and production of TruSweet, Sunrider's stevia product, were being terminated. The U.S. Food and Drug Administration apparently had categorized stevia as an unapproved artificial sweetener, even though it was an all-natural product and was used widely throughout the world as a substitute for sugar. Thousands of people by now were using and ordering this very popular Sunrider product. Drs. Chen and Black attempted to reason with the government officers. But the agents had no interest in discussing the matter. "Terminate distribution of the product," they informed Chen, "or we'll shut your company down."

In the middle of the excitement and enthusiasm of their convention, the Sunrider leaders met privately and debated what course to take. How would their distributors react to the loss of this very popular product? Having both the state and federal governments take such aggressive action against the company seemed to suggest that the company did not comply with government standards. The reputation and very credibility of Sunrider could be cast into doubt.

Chen decided that there was but one thing that he could and should do. He returned to the convention session and stood at the podium in front of the entire distributor body. With a sincere and very direct approach, he leveled with his distributors.

"Sunriders, we are facing a challenge. We have found ourselves in the unpleasant position of being pressured to terminate production of our stevia product. We have not been given specific reasons for this request. But we intend to cooperate fully with all regulatory agencies in an effort to demonstrate our good faith and our intention to obey all laws and regulations. At the same time, we will mount a very aggressive campaign and utilize every resource at our disposal to once again bring TruSweet to the marketplace."

"Please remember," he said, "the ancient Chinese did not have stevia, and it was not in my original health program. However, because it has been such a useful product and serves to naturally enhance our other products, it has been included in the Total Health Program."

Chen concluded, "Our mission remains the same. We are committed to promoting health and prosperity and to support the continued growth of each of your businesses. We now ask for your support in helping us to withstand these forces which would try to limit our success."

The crowd of distributors was both shocked and disappointed by Chen's message, but appreciated his honest approach. For many of them, much of their business had focused on promotion of the TruSweet product. The excitement and enthusiasm of the convention suddenly seemed to evaporate.

Within minutes, however, a new feeling swept over the crowd. What Sunrider represented was far more than

TruSweet. What had drawn thousands of people to Sunrider, including most of the distributors in the audience, had not been just an individual product, but Sunrider's basic concepts of health, its Philosophy of Regeneration, and the Total Health Program, which was based upon a foundation of creating balance in the body through the use of Nutrien and Calli Tea.

Even more compelling to the crowd had been Chen's honest and forthright manner in dealing with the distributors. Now he was asking for their support and understanding. The distributors in attendance had benefited greatly through Sunrider's products and marketing plan. Their loyalty was not something that they needed to think about, it was simply felt from the heart. To the best of Chen's knowledge, not a single Sunrider distributor left the company because of government problems with TruSweet.

True to Chen's word, Sunrider did mount a campaign and used every available resource to bring their stevia product back to the marketplace. It took thirteen years, tens of thousands of dollars, the passage of new federal legislation, and an initiative from federal regulators. But in July 1997, the U.S. Food and Drug Administration, based upon applications filed by Sunrider, authorized the production of stevia as a dietary supplement.

Sunrider proved its leadership in the herbal nutritional industry through supporting the Dietary Supplement Act of 1994 and through marshaling the approval of stevia through the FDA. Today, Sunrider proudly markets its stevia product under the names Sunny Dew and Sunectar, which are widely accepted as the finest stevia products available in the world. The TruSweet experience taught Chen an important lesson—when faced with a challenge, being forthright and direct with his distributors was the best approach.

∽

During Sunrider's first years of operation it became increasingly clear that the company would not only be successful but that success was coming on a far grander scale than anyone had dreamed possible. By 1985 sales volume exceeded the million-dollar mark and the surface had barely been scratched. The nearly unlimited potential of Sunrider's future was being realized by more people each day. The fruits of Sunrider's success became sweeter and sweeter.

Each month, hundreds of new distributors were being introduced to Sunrider's products as well as Sunrider's business opportunity. As they became converted to the products, they became increasingly willing to consider the financial opportunities of network marketing. Just as Sunrider knew that its products were of superior quality, Chen also hoped that the Sunrider distributor organization would recognize his compensation plan as being one of the most stable and generous in the industry. By 1986, dozens of distributors every month were purchasing new cars through their Sunrider income and incentives. Hundreds were traveling to exotic places to participate in Sunrider conventions.

Chen took the company profits and returned them into building the business. New construction began on manufacturing facilities while distributors began constructing new homes. Chen felt it was important to set an example for his distributors to follow. He dressed well and within a few years was able to buy a new Mercedes Benz. Actually he bought three—one for himself, one for his sister Jau-Hwa, and one for his parents. But as success grew, so did the divisiveness and distance between Chen and his parents. Just as Chen had not anticipated Sunrider's dramatic early successes, he had not considered the sharpness of the wedge that was being driven between him and his parents.

While Papa Chen in his heart desperately wanted to celebrate his son's good fortune, by virtue of Chen's success the elder Chen had lost face—at least within his family. After all, it was Papa Chen who had been adamantly opposed to the creation of Sunrider. It was Papa Chen who had laughed at and derided his son for even thinking that a young Chinese man could successfully sell herbs in America. And it was Papa Chen who had refused to lend his son any financial support in pursuit of his dream. Tei Fu had been proven right. Papa Chen had been proven wrong. In the traditional Chinese culture, the son should not embarrass the father, even if that was never Chen's intention.

Tei Fu believed that it was difficult for Papa Chen to see him succeeding as an entrepreneur when every business venture that the elder Chen had undertaken had either failed or been disappointing. The dramatic gains of Sunrider daily reminded Papa Chen of the pain and rejection he had felt as a young man when his step-brother had been so successful in launching his electronics business while he, Yung-Yeuan Chen, toiled as a government worker. The elder Chen had always harbored his own dream that someday he would come to America, that he would develop a "big idea," and that he would pursue the American Dream. He was just as smart, just as capable, and just as hard working as either his step-brother or his son. It was difficult to accept that fate had enabled both of them to be successful in their ventures while he struggled with his.

Then there was the issue of the in-laws. While both Mama and Papa Chen admired Oi-Lin's accomplishments, especially that she was a medical doctor, they couldn't help but compare Oi-Lin's station in life to that of their own daughters. With her husband, Oi-Lin seemed to be amassing what their own children could not. And it was Oi-Lin's extended family who was participating in the financial success of Sunrider, not the Chen family. Oi-Lin's father, through his initial investment with Tei Fu, was in a position to achieve huge financial gain. The Tsui family had created their own company, called Paget, which Chen had agreed could play the primary role in acquiring the raw herbs which Sunrider would need as the ingredients in its products, and in processing the herbs before they could be formulated and manufactured.

Jealousy was apparent. In his interaction with Tei Fu and Oi-Lin, Papa Chen became increasingly difficult. He constantly felt the need to reassert himself as the dominant one, the authority figure, the patriarch in control. Even on simple issues there seemed to be conflict. If the family was eating at a restaurant and Tei Fu picked up the tab, he might leave a ten-dollar tip on the table. The elder Chen would snatch up the ten-dollar bill, replace it with a five, and then chide his son for not being more frugal. There was an increasing level of resentment shown toward Oi-Lin as well. No longer did her parents-in-law ask about her medical practice. Privately they whispered that they were embarrassed she had not received her degree from a more prestigious medical school. They couldn't understand why she felt the need to pursue her own profession if her husband was to be successful in his. In the mid-'80s the Chens had four small children, all of whom were beautiful, and who through Sunrider's success would have uncommon opportunity for the rest of their lives. Their grandparents seemed cool toward them, and the normal bonding that occurs between grandparents and grandchildren was withheld.

The resentment of Mama and Papa Chen was reflected in small but cutting ways. One day as Oi-Lin was changing the diaper on her youngest child, Sunny, there erupted a debate over whether Oi-Lin should use disposable diapers. "What makes you so special?" her parents-in-law asked. "Cloth diapers are cheaper. You're not above the rest of us. You should wash your children's diapers just like the rest of us have always done." Oi-Lin didn't know how to respond. But it would make no difference. The bitterness felt by her husband's parents was not something that would be resolved through reasoning and understanding.

From Papa Chen's point of view, order had to be re-established within the family. Face had to be restored. It wasn't to be an issue of whether his son bought him a new car or a new home. It was more an issue of whether the younger Chen would obey his father regardless of what the father wanted in return. That was the Chinese tradition that had endured for thousands of years. That was the way that

Yung-Yeuan had treated his father. That was the way of Confucius.

∾

In late 1984, nearly two years after Sunrider had been founded, the ownership and leadership of Sunrider became vested solely in Tei Fu Chen's hands. Dean Black had functioned as president of Sunrider and Tei Fu as CEO. Black had a small ownership in Sunrider, which he said "Chen gave me out of the goodness of his heart."

Black had contributed greatly to Sunrider's early success, but was not comfortable as a businessman or administrator. He was a student and a scholar. Like his friend, Tei Fu, his first love was studying philosophy. He enjoyed writing and lecturing, but managing the day-to-day affairs of a rapidly growing network marketing company was not the highest or best use of Black's intellectual and writing skills. He and Chen agreed that he would be more focused and could better contribute to Sunrider's success outside rather than inside the company. Black subsequently sold all of his stock back to Chen.

Chen encouraged Black to run for Congress. He felt the American government could use someone with Black's depth of thought and understanding of where the future should head in health care. Black laughed at Chen's suggestion, realizing he was no more of a politician than he was a salesman. Instead, Black chose to write books, including one entitled *Health With a Chinese Twist*. Black's book eventually sold several hundred thousand copies, and when he attended a Sunrider convention in August of the following year he was treated as a celebrity. Sunrider distributors not only loved Black's book, but because of his character and wisdom he was deeply respected by all who knew him.

Through the years, Dean Black and Tei Fu Chen have maintained a close relationship and mutual respect. "Chen once told me that Sunrider's strength was in his [Chen's] mind," says Black. "To Chen, Sunrider was much more than a business and much more than his dream. It was his *vision* and *purpose*. Sunrider overcame many obstacles by virtue of Chen's sheer courage and will to go on. I've seen him weep under the agony and pressure of all of the adversity that he has faced, but he just kept on going. He sees his destiny as something much bigger than himself. He believes that Sunrider came about with a purpose. Through the years I've talked to Chen about almost every situation he has faced. I've never seen him bitter. The greatest challenge that he has ever faced through the years has been with his family. And even then I've never seen him bitter. Just sad."

CHAPTER TWELVE

California Sun

As Sunrider approached its fourth anniversary, the success of the company and its phenomenal growth had exceeded all hopes and expectations. Tei Fu characterized Sunrider's success as "a dream come true." That was an understatement. Tens of thousands of people had embraced Chen's "Philosophy of Regeneration." Sunrider was selling its products as fast as they could be manufactured. Hundreds of new distributors were signing up every day.

The "Total Health Program" consisted of the Sunergy line of Nutrien, the formulation representing Yin herbs which provided basic herbal nutrition to the body; Calli Tea, the "Yang formulation" which helped to naturally cleanse the body's systems of wastes and toxins; and the Quinary formulations, based upon the Chinese concept of the "five elements," designed to nourish and create harmony among the body's five primary health systems. A body that was balanced, with its five systems working in harmony, can enjoy the greatest health. The Synergy line was conveniently packaged in what was called a Sunpack.

Sunrider also introduced a weight management system which was called the Vitalite line, offered, appropriately enough, in a Slimpack; and the Kandesn line of skin care and beauty products to promote healthy skin and a youthful, natural beauty.

Sunrider's early distributors followed a consistent pattern of conversion to the company. Most were intrigued by the Chinese philosophies as taught by Tei Fu Chen, so they tried the products. The products typically made a very real, and in many cases immediate, impact upon people's health and appearance. For most users the results were simply undeniable. Their enthusiasm for the products motivated consumers to talk to their friends, family, and work associates about their Sunrider discovery. In the process of introducing the product to others, they also discovered the Sunrider business opportunity, offering the potential to make a great deal of money. In fact, through bonuses and commissions, Sunrider paid back to its distributors nearly 40 percent of its total sales volume. As Sunrider's sales volume grew into the tens of millions of dollars, many Sunrider distributors began earning incomes which created lifestyles dramatically improved from what they previously had known or thought possible.

New cars and homes were suddenly within reach. Most distributors worked part-time. Hundreds of others made a Sunrider career a full-time pursuit.

One Sunrider leader characterized his experience this way: "Sunrider gave me and my wife the financial independence to, in a very real sense, be *free*. I felt liberated. For the first time in my life I felt like I could get up in the morning and do exactly what *I wanted to do*. And what I was doing was meeting with and helping other people. I actually felt that I was touching other people's lives in such a personal and positive way. So beyond the power of freedom that I had found, I had also discovered a tremendous *sense of purpose*."

Sunrider created a lifestyle that was exciting and enticing. Leadership meetings for Sunrider's top-ranking distributors were held every January, either in Hawaii or aboard cruise ships. The Sunrider family enjoyed training and parties as they glided through the sparkling waters of the Caribbean and along the coasts of Mexico. Getaways were held in resorts such as Park City, Utah, where Tei Fu Chen conducted two- or three-day training seminars exploring new ways Sunrider and its leaders could expand their phenomenal growth potential. Summer conventions were held for Sunrider mainstream distributors in Los Angeles, Salt Lake City, Calgary, New York, Chicago, and Honolulu.

Tei Fu spent most of his life on airplanes traveling from city to city, meeting to meeting. "I remember giving a lecture in Seattle soon after the company was formed," he says. "At that time, I would travel to a different city nearly every night to talk about Sunrider, our philosophy, and our unique herbal formulations. Sometimes I would schedule two meetings in one night and it was very easy to become fatigued.

"When I arrived at a lecture in Seattle I was so tired that I didn't know whether I could make it through my entire presentation. When I walked into the meeting room, however, a little girl ran up to me with a big smile and hugged my legs. 'Thanks Dr. Chen,' she said, 'You helped make me better.'

"I was so touched. The products really did seem to be making a difference in people's lives. Our purpose wasn't healing, but helping people find health. That thought alone energized me and kept me going night after night."

Building Sunrider through the early 1980s was not an easy task for Chen. He still struggled with the English language and was often frustrated in trying to communicate

clearly with people. Owning his own business required that
he work long into the nights, sometimes packaging the
Sunrider products, and other times marketing them. Tei Fu
alone did all of the research and development work, constantly experimenting with new formulas and creating new
products. As if that were not a full-time job, he also had to
work with hundreds of Sunrider distributors to expand the
distributor network.

Chen lacked experience in many areas, and simply had
to learn as he went. As one person put it, "Chen had a great
recipe for lasagna, but he didn't know how to prepare it for
10,000 people." Consequently, he traveled often to Asia to
meet with his father-in-law who was much more experienced in the sourcing and manufacturing of herbs and who
became an indispensable source of support to Chen. By
1983 the demand for Sunrider herbs had grown to the
point that Tei Fu felt he needed to work out a more formal
arrangement with his father-in-law. He asked Papa Tsui to
work on a full-time basis sourcing the herbs, making sure
they were of the highest quality, arranging for the initial
manufacturing, overseeing the quality control systems at
the manufacturing facilities, and guarding the secrecy of the
formulas.

Papa Tsui set up a Hong Kong facility under the ownership of a company he created called Paget Enterprises. Oi-
Lin's brother, Man Tat, joined his father at Paget while Oi-
Lin's sister, May-Lin, helped supervise the new Paget
warehouse in Hong Kong. Chen agreed to pay his father-
in-law a fixed price per kilo for the processed herbs, and in
that way Tei Fu could establish a stable price for his herbal

products in America. Depending upon the herbs, the weather, and market demands, prices for raw herbs fluctuate quite dramatically. Tei Fu did not want to constantly be changing the prices of his products. The "fixed price" arrangement was fair to both Sunrider and to Chen's in-laws at Paget. He realized that without his father-in-law's support and involvement, Sunrider would never be in a position to flourish. He wished that his own father had been willing to play a greater role.

Tei Fu made many attempts to involve his own family in the Sunrider organization. The effort proved more difficult than he had anticipated. His older sister Sheue Wen, and younger sister Jau-Fang, had both married and were living out of the state. Jau-Fei was studying at BYU and was not interested in a part-time job. Chen's father also showed surprisingly little interest. At times he would offer his son advice and direction. Generally, however, Papa Chen remained skeptical of Sunrider's success and kept himself safely distanced from his son's "risky" company.

Jau-Hwa, then twenty-six, was the only member of the Chen family willing to join with her brother. Tei Fu made his sister his executive assistant. After Dean Black's departure in 1984, Jau-Hwa took on more and more responsibility for building on Sunrider's growth, overseeing many of the day-to-day business operations for the company.

She supervised the Sunrider staff and played a primary role with distributors, making sure their products and checks were delivered to them in a timely manner. Tei Fu remained focused on developing new product formulations, and was forced to spend a great deal of time on the road,

meeting with distributors and teaching his Philosophy of
Regeneration.

By 1986 Sunrider had enjoyed such success that Tei Fu
spent an afternoon at a Mercedes Benz dealership, where he
bought three new Mercedes 560 SELs—one for him and
Oi-Lin, one for Jau-Hwa, and one for his parents. Sunrider's Auto Fund had also enabled dozens of Sunrider distributors to purchase new automobiles. The opportunity to
finally buy the fine cars for himself and his family gave Tei
Fu a great sense of accomplishment. The fruits of Sunrider's
success were being enjoyed by thousands of people. Chen
felt he, too, should be entitled to enjoy a sweet bite of the
Sunrider fruit.

❧

Nineteen eighty-six was also a year of tragedy. Oi-Lin's
beloved father, Papa Tsui, died as the result of a stroke
brought on by hypertension that had plagued him
throughout his adult life. He was sixty-eight years old.

His death began a chain of events that would greatly
affect all associated with Sunrider for years to come. Oi-
Lin's brother, Man-Kwong, had also died the year before at
the relatively young age of thirty-five from cancer. Papa
Tsui's estate was left to be split among the surviving children: Oi-Lin, Man Tat, and May-Lin. Since Oi-Lin and
May-Lin were the daughters of the family, Tei Fu encouraged his brother-in-law, Man Tat, to continue with the
operations of Paget. He was doing a good job and had
played a key role in Sunrider's success.

Using standard financial computations, it was determined that Paget was worth approximately ten times its annual profit of about $4 million, which created a total worth of about $40 million. In exchange for taking full ownership of Paget, Man Tat agreed to pay each of his sisters $13 million. Since the chunky former fry cook obviously did not have that level of cash reserves available, Oi-Lin and Tei Fu agreed that when the time arose to claim Oi-Lin's inheritance fund, they would work out a more detailed arrangement with Man Tat.

On Tei Fu's side of the family, Jau-Hwa continued to do an outstanding job of managing the day-to-day affairs of Sunrider. Distributors felt a great affection for her. "She was like our own daughter," said Sunrider distributor Grey Jensen. "We loved that gal."

Jau-Hwa seemed to have everything going for her. She was young, beautiful, and talented at running the company with a firm hand. Tei Fu and his sister got along well until the death of Oi-Lin's father. Tei Fu's parents felt that Man Tat had been given a very rich deal for the role that Paget played in the importation and the processing of Sunrider herbs. His parents resented the fact that Oi-Lin's side of the family was profiting far more from the success of Sunrider than Chen's immediate family. They seemed to forget that it was Papa Tsui who had invested in Sunrider at the outset, and taken his share of risks.

Chen was constantly criticized by his parents for not showing filial piety to Papa Chen by taking better care of his sisters. Chen understood, at least in part, the reasons for his parents' resentment. They couldn't speak English. They never read an English-language newspaper or understood

American television or radio. Through their years in Brazil and then in Utah, their only source of outside information had been from their interpreters with whom they shared their home—Jau-Hwa and Jau-Fei. Both sisters harbored resentment, and felt strongly that they deserved a larger slice of the pie of their brother's success.

Through the years, Jau-Hwa particularly seemed to grow more resentful, especially toward Oi-Lin and her family. As the company controller, Jau-Hwa saw every invoice that Paget sent in, and the large amounts of money that were transferred from Sunrider to Paget. She felt that Tei Fu's in-laws were being favored. Although she never said anything directly to Tei Fu about her frustrations, rumors circulated among the family and through that feedback, Tei Fu believed Jau-Hwa regularly vented her disgruntlement to her parents and her sister Jau-Fei.

One thing was certain: Mama Chen was not going to be satisfied if her youngest daughter was to be forced into the shadow of Oi-Lin Chen.

∽

Near the end of 1985, Tei Fu was conducting a meeting in Los Angeles with a large group of distributors and new prospects in attendance. Following the meeting, Tei Fu felt impressed that the company should move its headquarters to Southern California. He had been traveling to the Los Angeles area often to hold meetings. Now was the time, he felt, to be there on a full-time basis. More than just a rational thought, he felt a deeper impression, much as he had when he envisioned the name and logo for Sunrider.

Pragmatically, Los Angeles obviously was a far better hub for international expansion than Provo, Utah. The Los Angeles International Airport was the gateway to the world. Tei Fu and Oi-Lin wanted Sunrider to become more cosmopolitan and to demonstrate their commitment to their distributors to take Sunrider to the "next level." Being based in Los Angeles would mean playing in the big leagues, but Tei Fu felt that both he and his company were prepared.

Making the move to California would not be easy. Chen had just purchased a fifteen-acre lot in the Provo/Orem area and had arranged for a $2 million bank loan to build a new manufacturing plant. But his determination to open a new chapter for Sunrider in Southern California was not to be deterred. He canceled the bank loan, arranged to sell the property, and along with Oi-Lin began preparations to find both a house and a headquarters in the Los Angeles area.

The Chens considered living in many of Southern California's more popular communities including Beverly Hills, Newport Beach, and Long Beach. Eventually they settled upon an area called Palos Verdes—a quiet hillside community south of the Los Angeles airport which overlooked the majestic South Bay and Pacific Ocean. It was not as flashy as other areas they had considered, such as Beverly Hills, but they felt that it would be a great place to raise a family, in part because of the many excellent schools in the area.

Some had speculated that the Chens would buy a beautiful mansion on a hilltop. Such a home would eventually come. But for the time being they needed their money to build Sunrider's headquarters and new manufacturing facilities. Just before Christmas 1986, rather than buying a house, the Chens rented a place in Palos Verdes.

As a location for their corporate headquarters, Torrance was particularly attractive because it was only a few minutes from their home and a short fifteen-minute drive to the airport, making it very accessible for employees, for distributors, and for traveling guests.

Oi-Lin concluded an important chapter in her life when she closed her medical practice in Orem. She had made plans to get her medical license in California and open a new practice in Palos Verdes. Her goal was not to be realized. Oi-Lin had agreed to oversee construction of the new corporate headquarters in Torrance while Tei Fu commuted between Utah and Los Angeles for nearly seven months. Tei Fu immediately began the planning and design of a huge 188,000 square-foot state-of-the-art manufacturing plant in nearby City of Industry. In the meantime, the Orem manufacturing plant was kept operational until the California facility could be completed. Oi-Lin had her hands full, rearing a large family that had now grown to five children with the birth of Jonathan in October 1984, and managing the building of the impressive new world headquarters of Sunrider International on Lomita Boulevard. Her days of practicing medicine were over.

Before the Orem facility was closed, calamity struck. From Sunrider's inception, Nutrien, its flagship product, was formulated using a protein-rich soy base along with Dr.

Chen's exclusive formulation of herbs. Soy was an ideal base because of its high protein and because it dissolves easily when mixed with liquid. Soy also spoils easily, and is a hospitable host to hungry bacteria.

Sunrider has never in its history used preservatives or other artificial ingredients in its products. Neither does the company use chemicals or radiation to sterilize any products. The ability to produce nutrient-rich herbal foods that are virtually free from bacteria or any other form of contaminant is one discipline that sets Sunrider apart from almost every other herbal manufacturer. Most of Sunrider's competitors simply grind up raw herbs and dehydrate and package them. Sunrider manufactures herbal concentrates that are pure and preservative-free.

But Sunrider's exclusive approach to manufacturing nearly destroyed the company during its fifth year of operation. The California Health Department routinely inspected the new company in Torrance and took samples of products from the "returned product section," an area where trash was being discarded. It tested positive for the salmonella bacteria. Upon notifying Sunrider of their findings, Tei Fu faced a difficult decision. He could try to deal with the regulators privately, correct the problem and likely pay a fine, or he could deal with the challenge in a more public way. Chen decided if Sunrider was to maintain its reputation for high quality and integrity, problems must be dealt with in a manner that would be beyond reproach.

Sunrider immediately terminated the Nutrien product line and issued a voluntary recall of Nutrien, even though the government had not required such action.

There was no evidence that the salmonella contamination was in any of the Sunrider products, or that the contamination extended beyond the small area where the waste products had been discarded.

Many of Chen's distributor leaders felt that he was overreacting. Product recall was an extreme and very public measure. But in Chen's mind, although the recall could cause the company to suffer for the short term, in the long term consumers would be assured that the company would do whatever was necessary to produce products they could trust completely.

The recall cost the company several million dollars. It was very unlikely that any consumer had become ill from eating Nutrien. There was no report of anyone getting sick from eating Nutrien.

Later, Chen developed an improved formula called NuPlus to replace Nutrien. Reflecting upon the experience, he said, "When you get knocked down you just have to stand back up and continue on your way. Put the shadow behind you."

As far as Dr. Chen was concerned, Sunrider had made a mistake. The company did everything in its power to correct it. It was time to move on. State officials, however, saw it as an opportunity to pat themselves on the back publicly, and the discovery of the contamination was played up in the media for weeks.

Subsequently, when Sunrider announced plans to possibly move its manufacturing facilities to California, the Utah regulators became effusive in their praise. Sunrider was "a good corporate citizen" and "consistently showed the highest levels of cooperation with health officials." Sun-rider was "to be praised for utilizing manufacturing processes that demonstrate superior quality controls."

But others, intent on attacking or destroying Sunrider, paid no attention to the praise of Utah regulators, or to the expensive and voluntary efforts undertaken by the company to correct the problem. The exploiters and connivers had their own agendas for Sunrider. The salmonella issue gave them the ammunition they needed, and in both California and Utah, Sunrider and its founder Tei Fu Chen were in their gun sights.

Proud parents bring home Wendy, their first child—Provo, Utah, November 1974.

Tei Fu, Oi-Lin, and Wendy at the apartment following their temple marriage sealing ceremony— Provo, Utah, February 1976.

Oi-Lin with daughter, Sunny, 1980.

Tei Fu at his parents' home in Orem, Utah.

Tei Fu and Oi-Lin showing off their first baby, Wendy, and their first car.

During their first years in America, when money was tight, Tei Fu caught fish for dinner in the Provo River.

Tei Fu and Oi-Lin, seven months pregnant, just before traveling to America, 1974.

Oi-Lin with daughter, Wendy, at Disneyland, 1975.

Tei Fu displays his judo trophies at BYU, 1975.

Tei Fu teaching martial arts at BYU, 1977.

Tei Fu, Oi-Lin and Wendy Chen are sealed in the
Provo LDS temple, February 1976.

The Chens with their landlords,
saying good-bye to Oi-Lin, seven
months pregnant at the time, 1974.

Tei Fu in Brazil, on his way to
the United States, 1974.

Tei Fu gets accustomed to life in America without
Oi-Lin—Yellowstone Park, 1975.

Tei Fu and Oi-Lin, pregnant with
Wendy in Taiwan, 1974.

Oi-Lin with two-year-old
Wendy, 1976.

The Chens enjoying their first trip to Hawaii, 1986.

The Chen family celebrating an American Christmas, 1982.

Oi-Lin with all five children, (left to right) Sunny, Jonathan, Wendy, Eric, Reuben, 1985.

Tei Fu in Sunrider lab at Orem, Utah facility.

Tei Fu and Oi-Lin at Sundance Ski
Resort, Utah—their first and last
ski trip.

The Chen family on vacation at
San Diego Zoo, February 1987.

Tei Fu spending family time with his children in Japan (left to right) Jonathan, Sunny, Eric.

Oi-Lin and daughter, Wendy— an autumn day in Utah, 1976.

Tei Fu with children, at home in Orem, Utah, 1985.

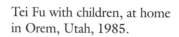

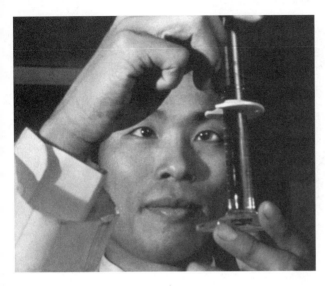

Tei Fu overseeing quality
control procedures.

A successful Tei Fu Chen, 1983.

Tei Fu at City of Industry research
and development lab.

Tei Fu speaks at an early
Sunrider seminar, 1983.

Tei Fu at Sunrider's
Utah office, 1983.

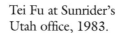

Sunrider's office and
manufacturing facilities in
Orem, Utah, 1984.

CHAPTER THIRTEEN

Sharks in the Water

$\mathcal{S}$uccess often brings out the best and worst in people and in politics. The TruSweet and salmonella issues had taught Tei Fu Chen a bit about the politics of government. With the scent of Sunrider's success still fresh in the water, another group of sharks began to gather. Tei Fu Chen was now going to learn the hard lessons of politics in the news media and the extraordinary power of the press, which can be used to either build or destroy.

Four times each year television stations determine their advertising rates based upon viewership of their programs during a particular month. February of 1988 was a "sweeps month" and the three local TV network affiliates in Salt Lake City were engaged in a fierce competition for ratings points. In the battle for advertising dollars, sometimes professional and objective news coverage takes a back seat to sensationalism and controversy.

KSL television had worked for months on a five-part "investigative series" that it launched in the heart of the ratings season, entitled "Herbal Medicine: Miracle or Mirage." A reporter named Con Psarras targeted Sunrider and more particularly Tei Fu Chen. Psarras would later comment, "Tei Fu Chen is a gracious, charming, and successful man who has lots of friends . . . and enemies." The content of the series suggested that Psarras had spent most of his time with the "enemies."

The story was introduced: "They [referring to Sunrider distributors] are a devoted army whose faith in the product, by their own admission, borders on the fanatic." Psarras gave a quick overview of the company, pointing out that it had become one of Utah's largest, with revenues over $100 million per year. "It's the kind of corporate success story you heard about in the 1970s. Sales double every six months and the number of customers tripled last year [1987]. It's a sleek operation. The company says it does things for your health other modern medicine can't do."

Part One featured Sunrider distributors who Psarras claimed often sold Sunrider products door-to-door as "miracle medicine"—able to treat and cure almost any disease. A video excerpt showed a distributor talking about her mother who had had cancer and who she felt was helped by Sunrider products. "It's testimonials like that, as opposed to scientific test, that the company relies on to show its products are effective," said Psarras. "There are lots of testimonials and lots of satisfied customers, and there have recently been some scientific tests too—last week the company was closed after finding salmonella poisoning." The *company*, of course, had not been closed.

Psarras then focused on Tei Fu Chen, founder of Sunrider International. Psarras called Chen "Something of a guru for the 15,000 people who call themselves Sunriders. They spread his gospel and praise his wisdom. There is an aura of success surrounding the man whom his followers call 'Dr. Chen.'" Psarras then challenged Tei Fu Chen's credentials, pointing out that Chen was not a medical doctor nor was he licensed as a pharmacist in California. Neither Chen's background as an herbologist nor his pharmaceutical training in Taiwan was discussed in the report.

The third segment discussed the athletic department at Brigham Young University where many athletes had been using Sunrider products. The department had asked BYU to conduct a formal study of the herbs, and samples of Sunrider products had been sent to a laboratory for analysis. BYU had received only preliminary results and refused to discuss their findings with Psarras. He persisted: "BYU isn't saying, but Probe Five has learned that these extensive tests found chemical substances in various Sunrider products that are similar to and may have the same effect as powerful prescription drugs." Psarras rhetorically asked: "Are these herbs providing a feeling of good health because they are improving nutrition or because they may be laced with chemicals that can artificially make you feel good?"

The investigative reporter then focused yet more attention on Sunrider distributors and consumers who touted the philosophy of the "miracle of regeneration." "Where is the evidence?" one doctor asked, and then answered, "It's ancient mumbo jumbo."

Referring to Sunrider distributors, Psarras said, "These people with stories of miracle cures also turn out to be usually the people who sell Sunrider products. Sunriders are overzealous, on the lookout for anyone who is sick." The reporter did explain that Sunrider strictly forbids its distributors from using the product to treat disease. "But whether the company frowns on it or not, the company still profits from it."

In the final segment of the series, KSL seemed to take a little more balanced approach. Psarras admitted that the TV station, during the week of the broadcast, had been overwhelmed with hundreds of phone calls from people who were satisfied users of Sunrider products. A spokesperson for Sunrider blasted the series: "You cannot pull the wool over so many eyes. Sunrider products are helping people in their day-to-day lives and people are sending the message by ordering more product and by telling their neighbors." Psarras reminded the Sunrider representative that "we have reported how in some cases distributors advertise for serious disease." The Sunrider spokesperson explained that the company does not desire to make money that way. "We actively discourage it, persistently and consistently . . . our products are exactly what we say they are—pure herbal products and nothing else."

Psarras concluded his week-long series by acknowledging the huge volume of telephone calls the station had received. "In the meantime, Sunrider users are telling us they remain devoted to the product. They say anything that makes them feel that good can't be bad."

It wasn't just KSL's phone ringing off the hook. Tei Fu Chen was receiving hundreds of phone calls from his distributors. They all asked him one question, "What can we do to help?"

A college student named Teena Horlacher, daughter of a Sunrider distributor, was so upset by the negative bias that had been shown to Sunrider in KSL's coverage that she conducted an investigation of her own as an assignment for an ethics class at Utah State University. She interviewed KSL reporter Con Psarras and news director Spence Kinnard and confronted them with hard evidence of their biased reporting. She pointed out that Psarras had consistently used loaded words and phrases that convey great emotion but little journalistic fact. Calling Sunrider distributors "an army" and "fanatics" and referring to Dr. Chen as a "guru" with a "gospel" implied that Sunrider was cult-like, rather than a professional business.

During Horlacher's interview with Psarras, she reported that he referred to Chen as a "guru," but quickly corrected himself, saying "I hate to refer to him [Chen] as that." Still, he had placed that image in the minds of hundreds of thousands of viewers.

The thousands of devoted and enthusiastic Sunrider distributors in Utah resented being portrayed as fanatics and zealots. They responded with a barrage of phone calls to the station in response to the series. Horlacher asked Psarras why he chose to portray only the negative side of a few distributors and did not portray any of the more typical distributors in a positive light. Psarras replied, "If fifty planes landed safely at the airport, would you report it?"

Even Dr. David B. Roll, a University of Utah professor of medicinal chemistry who earlier in the broadcast had been highly critical of some of Sunrider's distributors' selling tactics, told Horlacher that he felt the company had been improperly treated. "There were aspects of the report that were unfair to Sunrider. They [KSL] implied that the products contained prescription drugs that you would normally buy behind the counter, and there is no evidence to prove that," said the doctor. "Although I have no love for Sunrider, he [Psarras] had no evidence. Maybe I helped him in the jump in insinuating."

As for the products containing harmful substances,

Kinnard lamely explained, "We have no proof of this. We never said that it does have those things. Just that it *might* have those things."

Sunrider was anxious to have an opportunity to rebut many of the allegations that had been made during the KSL series. Accordingly, Sunrider purchased air time from the TV station to set the record straight. KSL agreed to sell the air time to Sunrider but provided strict guidelines which they insisted would have to be followed. Conforming to the guidelines, Sunrider quickly produced a brief video and delivered it to the station for broadcast. Shortly before it was scheduled to air, however, KSL contacted Sunrider, refusing to broadcast the piece and offering no explanation. The head of the sales department was more forthright than Psarras or Kinnard were willing to be. He explained that a management team had made a decision not to air the video, believing that it would likely damage KSL's credibility.

College student Teena Horlacher summarized her report on KSL with a sobering conclusion: "As a result of the unfair broadcast, Sunrider sales in Utah plunged from $1.2 million a month in January 1988 to about $400,000 a month following the broadcast of the series." What was only a bruise to Sunrider nationwide would prove to be devastating to the lives and livelihoods of hundreds of Sunrider distributors in Utah.

In part because of the KSL broadcast, Sunrider would eventually move its manufacturing facilities from Utah to California. It was a wise decision. For Sunrider to become an international force, it needed a global hub.

An article in the February 11, 1991 edition of the

Provo *Daily Herald* announced that Sunrider would be leaving Utah. "Sunrider Corporation, an herbal nutrient supplement and weight control product manufacturing company will close its doors next week because officials 'want out of Utah.' Closing the manufacturing facility February 22 will result in the layoff of 150 full-time employees and twenty part-time employees."

"'I think the main reason behind this is that they have set up a production plant in the City of Industry, California, with more advanced equipment,' Orem plant manager Steve Lee said."

The article in the *Herald* was followed by a letter to the editor by one of Utah's top distributors, Paul Jensen:

> A recent *Herald* article incorrectly implied that Sunrider International was leaving Utah. In fact, Utah continues to be one of the top ten states for Sunrider product distribution and growth. Sunrider is closing a *manufacturing facility* in Orem because the company recently completed its new City of Industry facility in California, one of the world's largest herbal processing plants. But Sunrider does continue to enjoy great success in Utah.
>
> Perhaps there's a message, however, in why Sunrider chose California for its state-of-the-art multi-million-dollar facility which will employ several hundred people.
>
> During the past eight years Sunrider has emerged as one of America's fastest-growing companies. Its founder, Tei Fu Chen, has been nominated as Entrepreneur of the Year. Company growth has exceeded $300 million. Thousands of Utahns generate income, jobs and tax revenues through Sunrider. Of Sunrider's nearly 500,000 distributors

throughout the world, six of the top distributors live right here in Utah. For a company that has done so much for Utah and its economy, Sunrider has been given little credit. The media have chosen to focus only on the negative, instead of the many positive accomplishments of this immensely successful Utah-born company.

Utah spends millions to attract new business to our state each year. It's a shame that we haven't learned how to treat fairly the ones that are already here.

Sincerely, Paul Jensen

Distributors were hurt. The Sunrider business was hurt. The Utah economy was damaged. All as a result of KSL's biased and damaging reporting.

It's hard to know how much the KSL broadcast influenced the actions of an Arizona real estate agent named Debi Boling, her attorney Mel McDonald, and her husband at the time, Ken Andrews. In the same month that the KSL series ran, Debi Boling filed a lawsuit, alleging that she had suffered severe hair loss, tooth discoloration, and flu-like symptoms, all as a result of consuming Sunrider herbal foods the previous year. Although Boling didn't mention in her initial documents which products she had eaten, she said she was confident that the Sunrider foods had caused her personal injuries.

Nearly two years after she filed suit, during the pre-trial stages of the litigation, Boling produced two canisters of what she claimed to be the very same Nutrien products she had consumed in 1987. The sample was chemically tested and was found to contain 5 percent lead. Experts on the case pointed out, however, that such a high lead content would likely kill a person and that lead contamination cannot cause hair loss. Miraculously, almost one year later, Boling came up with a second sample of Nutrien, again which she claimed to have consumed in 1987. She claimed that she had given the second canister of Nutrien to her former secretary who had fortuitously discovered its existence in June of 1990. The second sample of Nutrien was also tested and this one happened to contain 2.9 percent lead and 3 percent thallium. Experts were prepared to testify that thallium could in fact cause hair loss.

Dr. Chen knew immediately that he and Sunrider were being set up. During the 1980s, suing large and successful companies who cared about their public profile had become quite common. The number of fraudulent claims reached new record levels. Some cases, like the supposed syringe in a Pepsi can or the case of the tainted Tylenol, generated news headlines all over the world.

Chen knew that the Nutrien could not have been contaminated with lead for a number of reasons. First, there simply was no lead or lead derivatives such as lead acetate anywhere in Sunrider's manufacturing facilities. Since there was no lead on the property, how could lead have been mistakenly mixed into a batch of Nutrien? Second, since Sunrider products are mass produced in large batches and since a batch of Nutrien consists of 300 canisters, if one canister of Nutrien had lead in it, 299 others would have also. Third, every batch went through dozens of quality control tests and analyses. Every product that leaves the Sunrider manufacturing plant is chemically analyzed before and after it is placed in the final packaging containers. The Nutrien from the batch that Debi Boling alleged was contaminated had been through the Sunrider testing labs before it was shipped and Sunrider had the lab results and documentation to prove it.

The real issue wasn't how much lead or thallium was in the containers, how it got there, or where and by whom the contaminated product had been discovered. Boling's objective was not necessarily to win a court case. She, McDonald, and Andrews had but one purpose—to secure a multi-million-dollar settlement. Whether it came from a jury verdict or from a negotiated out-of-court settlement was hardly the issue. *They wanted money!* And their initial asking price was the nice round number of $10 million.

Their strategy was equally simple. Rather than focusing the suit on Debi Boling or on the Sunrider products for that matter, the spotlight would be focused on Tei Fu Chen. Rather than wait years for a jury verdict, they believed that by trying their case in the news media and attacking the reputation of Chen, his company, and his distributors, they could bring Tei Fu Chen to his knees and force a settlement through damaging publicity.

They also had an ace up their sleeve, although they likely didn't know it in February 1988. The ideal person to attack the credentials of Tei Fu Chen and of Sunrider wasn't an attorney or a plaintiff. The most credible accuser would be Tei Fu's own father, Yung-Yeuan Chen.

Chapter Fourteen

A House Divided

The fact that by 1988 Sunrider had grown to a $100 million company was not lost on Con Psarras. It was not lost on Debi Boling, and it certainly was on the mind of Papa Chen. Sunrider was making so much money that Tei Fu's father seemed to be embarrassed. Tei Fu had achieved what his father never could and what his mother had always wanted. Both parents had lost face. Tei Fu's mother also deeply resented the fact that Sunrider's newfound wealth had primarily benefited Oi-Lin's family.

Increasingly, when Tei Fu visited with his mother, her message was the same. "I raised you. Now you're successful. But what are you doing for your own family? What about your sisters? What about Jau-Fei?"

Papa Chen believed that he could save face and appease his wife by having his son do the proper thing—restore order in the Chen family. How? By making Yung-Yeuan (Papa Chen) chairman of Sunrider, Tei Fu the president, and splitting the company five ways, with 20 percent going to the father, 20 percent to the mother, 20 percent each to Jau-Fei and Jau-Hwa. Chen and Oi-Lin, together, would retain 20 percent. Yung-Yeuan said he would fairly redistribute Sunrider's earnings just like Grandpa Chen had done thirty years ago when Papa Chen had handed over his paycheck to him every week in Taiwan.

It was impossible for Tei Fu to give his father the company. He did not believe it was the right or fair thing to do. He told his father "No."

"But I gave my paycheck to your grandfather every week," Yung-Yeuan responded. "Now where is your respect?"

Tei Fu tried to appease his parents by assuring them that he would always take care of them. He would buy them cars and homes and provide the financial backing for their own business if that's what they chose to do.

Chen never actually expressed this feeling to his parents, but he thought it often: "You refused to help me. You told me that I would fail. Now why should I be expected to give up the company that I have worked so hard for, especially to *you*, who always doubted me!"

But Chen's parents persisted. Every time he saw them for a Sunday dinner or whenever they called on the telephone, they would repeat their demand that he hand over Sunrider. The last time he had such a conversation with his parents he responded that since Jau-Fei was now married, she should do what he, Tei Fu, had to do when he graduated from college—find a job. If Jau-Fei wanted money, perhaps she and her husband, Rui-Kang Zhang, should start their own business.

A few hours later, Chen's mother called back and said, "OK, we will do it ourselves." Tei Fu clearly understood what she meant. His parents and Jau-Fei planned to start their own business. He had no idea that it would be a competing herbal products company!

Without Tei Fu's knowledge, Jau-Fei and her father created a company in late 1987 called E. Excel. The elder Chen asked his son for a million dollars to support his retirement. Tei Fu asked his younger sister Jau-Hwa to wire a million dollars from Sunrider's cash reserves to their father. "I asked my dad that he not use the money against Sunrider in any way or to start a competing firm," Chen said. "He had always given me advice, so I considered the million dollars a consultant's fee."

Records show that the check likely ended up in an account at Central Bank in Provo, Utah, held by both Chen's father and his sister Jau-Fei—a fund which was used for doing E. Excel business.

In late 1987, as soon as she had received her Ph.D. in microbiology from BYU, Jau-Fei Chen created E. Excel. Tei Fu believed that E. Excel was to be involved in the business of importing latex gloves from China. Unbeknown to him, E. Excel was to become both a competitor and a nemesis to Sunrider.

The AIDS scare in the 1980s had created a shortage of rubber gloves in the United States. Surgical gloves were routinely worn by the workers at Sunrider's manufacturing facilities and Tei Fu was having a difficult time finding a stable source of supply. Rui-Kang, Jau-Fei's husband who had grown up in Shanghai, informed Tei Fu that he knew of glove suppliers in China whom he could contact.

Rui-Kang was a singer who had moved to America to attend BYU after performing with a Shanghai dancing and singing group that toured the United States. As a vocalist, he had met Jau-Fei when she had played piano accompaniment for one of his performances.

Neither Jau-Fei nor Rui-Kang had much meaningful business experience when E. Excel was created. Tei Fu had grave doubts about the future of their new business enterprise. Nevertheless, Tei Fu was in need of rubber gloves, so he asked his brother-in-law to research the costs to obtain gloves from the Chinese manufacturers and report back to him.

Upon Tei Fu's return from an overseas trip, he was surprised to learn that in his absence his sister, Jau-Hwa, Sunrider's controller, had already sent Rui-Kang a check for $500,000. Oi-Lin had approved the check because Jau-Hwa had given assurances that Tei Fu had authorized the transaction.

Upon seeing the prices for the gloves in the contract Rui-Kang had signed, Chen hit the roof. The prices were outrageously high. He immediately contacted the manufacturer in China to renegotiate the deal. Not only were costs way too high, he explained, but he needed only a few thousand dollars worth of gloves, not millions of them.

The manufacturer in China would not budge. In fact, he advised Chen that the initial $500,000 was only a down payment, and another $500,000 was due before any gloves would be shipped. Chen told Rui-Kang that he, Chen, was out of the deal. There was no point in throwing good money after bad, Chen had concluded. It would be best to just walk away and take his losses. Never again, he resolved, would he put himself in the position of doing business with his brother-in-law. His mother could protest all she wanted. Chen simply couldn't afford to further invest in the wild notions of the unskilled and inexperienced "businessman" Rui-Kang.

Because of AIDS, not only had the demand for rubber gloves soared but the U.S. Food and Drug Administration had substantially raised the quality standards for latex gloves—most of which were being used routinely in all medical fields as protection from potentially contaminated blood.

U.S. manufacturers, realizing the growing market demand, geared up production and became increasingly capable of meeting the needs of the American market.

While most of the foreign glove manufacturers met FDA standards, many others did not. With U.S. manufacturers expanding production, foreign suppliers were put at a disadvantage. The boxes of the E. Excel gloves were all clearly labeled "Made in China." From a marketing perspective, the Chinese labels were likely the kiss of death.

Unable to sell the gloves and still owing money for most of them, Jau-Fei and Rui-Kang faced a difficult dilemma. It was decided to print new sets of labels to cover the "Made in China" label. The new label said "Packaged, Sterilized, and Manufactured by E. Excel International, Provo, Utah." Exactly who made the decision was unclear. The finger-pointing would come later, as would the explanations which would be presented in front of a U.S. District Court judge.

A Salt Lake City television station, KUTV, reported the story on May 24, 1990:

The anchor lead-in said: "U.S. Customs agents say they seized millions of surgical gloves in Utah County. The gloves belonged to a Provo company being investigated by a grand jury. KUTV's Mary Sawyers is here to explain." Sawyers then reported:

> The U.S. Attorney's office confirms it is investigating a company called E. Excel out of Provo for allegedly mislabeling boxes containing seventeen million surgical gloves. Customs agents say it is one of the biggest seizures in surgical

gloves ever. It took them nine days to move the gloves into this storage shed. The rest sit in back in semi-trailers. The gloves were taken from the Provo company, clearly labeled "Packaged, Sterilized and Manufactured by E. Excel International, Provo, Utah." But sources say they were not made here. They were made in China. Only the offices and warehouses are in Provo. After the AIDS scare, medical and emergency personnel demanded more gloves than domestic makers could supply. Foreign companies flooded the market with gloves, many of poor quality. When hospitals started noticing the flaws, they began refusing gloves made outside of the U.S. This letter, "Intermountain Health Care," tells a foreign producer it will not buy latex gloves. The preference for use, it says, is clearly with domestic manufacturers. E. Excel's company president, Jau-Fei, refused an on-camera interview.

The grand jury returned felony indictments of both Jau-Fei and E. Excel on fraud and customs charges. On October 29, 1992, Jau-Fei reached a plea bargain with the Utah U.S. Attorney to plead guilty to reduced charges. She agreed to forfeit all of the latex gloves that had been seized in January 1990 and paid the U.S. Customs Service $178,401.

The terms of the negotiated settlement did not deal with the issue of whether she would be required to serve time in jail. That issue would be left up to Judge J. Thomas Greene who was scheduled to sentence her on January 4, 1993.

Prior to her appearance before Judge Greene, Jau-Fei's attorneys collected letters of personal reference from six of her employees, associates, and attorneys. The letters all pleaded for leniency and carried common themes justifying her behavior. One letter said, "She was a babe in the woods when it came to worldly affairs." Another talked of her lack of experience: "She unknowingly made unwise marketing decisions—based partially upon a general lack of business experience." Another talked of watching her "cry like a child and in her sobbing state, asking 'but what did I do wrong?'"

All of the letters pointed to a single individual, one Mickey Cochran, as the *real* culprit in the case. Wrote one attorney: "I believe that Jau-Fei became involved in the illegal packaging of the gloves because of her misplaced trust in a prominent member of her church." Another said, "It is very logical, I think, for her to believe upon the advice of a friend, especially if he is a religion teacher at her school." Her brother-in-law repeated the same thing, blaming her actions "upon the remarkably poor advice of her university religion professor." Jau-Fei's attorney, Stephen Hard, implied that her brother Tei Fu was somehow responsible. "Jau-Fei and her husband were thrust into the glove importation business when her brother, Tei Fu Chen, requested assistance in that field." Hard also pointed the finger of blame at the individual who "was a former religion instructor for the Mormon church. As a convert to that religion, Jau-Fei trusted Mr. Cochran and the advice he gave her."

In Jau-Fei's letter to Judge Greene, she was willing to assume at least part of the blame. "It was my responsibility to be sure E. Excel and myself were in compliance with all of the laws and regulations. I failed in this responsibility when I relied upon the advice of a religion teacher, Mickey Cochran."

Although Cochran was offered up by E. Excel and Jau-Fei's references as the person primarily responsible for the fraudulent scheme, he was never charged with any crime. Jau-Fei, however, was ordered to pay a fine and E. Excel was put on probation. The plea bargain marked the end of the "rubber gloves case" for E. Excel. Sunrider was to learn, however, that Mickey Cochran had been much more than a religious instructor and an advisor to Jau-Fei Chen. The name "Mickey Cochran" would surface again, not in the context of the rubber gloves case, but in the Debi Boling case.

In his letter to Judge Greene, attorney Stephen Hard acknowledged what Tei Fu had long suspected—that E. Excel had not been created with the purpose of being in the surgical glove importing basis. As Hard explained, referring to the 1988-1989 time frame, "During the same period, Jau-Fei's energies were primarily directed towards the development of E. Excel's principal, and now sole business, the formulation, manufacturing and marketing of herbal health food products."

The creation of E. Excel was an extremely bitter blow to Chen. "My sister never called to explain to me any of her plans. My parents said nothing. They stood beside me at the grand opening of our new headquarters on Lomita Boulevard in 1987, at the very same time that they were creating E. Excel. They acted happy. They seemed proud of me. I obviously had no idea of what was really going on, on the *inside*."

"It was a shock," echoed Oi-Lin, "My husband was very emotional. After all, it was his family turning against him."

CHAPTER FIFTEEN

Piercing
the Heart

*E*verything that E. Excel did in the early years seemed designed to imitate Sunrider. For five years, Sunrider had talked about combining 7,000 years of Chinese wisdom and tradition with Western science and technology. In E. Excel's first corporate profile, Jau-Fei said, "We have combined over 5,000 years of Chinese herbal lore with the most current research and technology to develop our unique line of natural health products." From the beginning, Chen had talked about achieving optimum health by promoting balance in the human body. The concepts of Yin and Yang were the bases around which all Sunrider products had been developed. In an E. Excel brochure Jau-Fei explained, "Illness is believed to be caused by an imbalance within the body: Thus the Chinese fundamental approach to health is to promote balance in the body. This balance is achieved through the interaction of opposing life-giving forces. The Chinese refer to these forces as Yin and Yang."

Sunrider had always promoted the value of whole foods such as herbs, rather than chemical isolates. Tei Fu often used the example of an orange as compared to vitamin C, or citric acid, to illustrate his point. Jau-Fei talked of the importance of using whole foods in nutrition and said, "For example, when vitamin C, or citric acid, is isolated from the orange, it becomes an element or chemical. Vitamin C is not an orange. An orange is a whole food with all the necessary elements present. It is more nutritious in its whole form than any single one of its elements."

Sunrider had set itself apart based on concentration and superior quality of its products. Sunrider used only the finest of herbs, and controlled its own manufacturing processes. E. Excel's approach once again mirrored Sunrider's. "E. Excel uses only the best and strongest herbs for formulations. The most nutritious parts of each herb are harvested and then concentrated . . . these herbs are then blended using the ancient philosophy of health and the technology of the modern world."

Chen was mostly flabbergasted, but a little flattered that his sister had so blatantly attempted to copy Sunrider's identity. "Don't people realize," Chen thought, "that when you try and copy someone else, the most you can ever hope for is to be number two?"

As long as E. Excel seemed intent on trying to copy Sunrider, Tei Fu Chen did not feel overly concerned. It would be impossible for his sister to duplicate the formulas of his products. Sunrider and Sunrider alone promoted the Philosophy of Regeneration. Chen had spent a lifetime devoted to the study of herbs. Jau-Fei was the new kid on the block.

She openly admitted her lack of herbal knowledge in a 1989 interview with the Provo *Daily Herald*. "I don't have all the knowledge about herbs," she said, adding that she was working with Chinese consultants to create her product formulations. "I feel I have to consult."

In the same interview Jau-Fei showed no reluctance in going head-to-head with her brother's company. "This is what I do best. I should have the freedom to start my own business and to compete in the free enterprise system."

E. Excel distributors also actively portrayed E. Excel products as nearly identical to Sunrider's. In a comparison chart, E. Excel distributors pointed out that Sunrider had NuPlus. E. Excel countered with Nutriall. Sunrider had Assimilaid, E. Excel offered Digeston. Sunrider had Meta-balance 44, E. Excel provided True Balance. Sunrider had a Hair Tonic 101, E. Excel matched it with a Herba Hair Tonic 108. Sunrider promoted Dong Quai caps and E. Excel promoted Dong Quai caps.

The comparisons and similarities did not end with products and philosophies. E. Excel's packaging, promotional materials, marketing plans, and distributor training all seemed to be created after Sunrider's likeness.

But try as she might, some things Jau-Fei could not copy. By 1990, Chen had invested over $100 million into research, development and manufacturing facilities. No other herbal manufacturer, and certainly not E. Excel, could promise, much less deliver, what Sunrider had already done. They could use Sunrider's promotional literature. They could package their products to resemble Sunrider's. But there was no way that what was inside the package was identical to what Sunrider was producing. In the absence of her own manufacturing capabilities, Jau-Fei was buying her herbal products from manufacturers in China and then repackaging them under the E. Excel label.

But Tei Fu came to believe that the plan of his parents and sister was far more deliberative and complex than simply trying to copy Sunrider. The first step *was* to imitate Sunrider. The second step was to attack it. And just like KSL and Debi Boling, their plan of attack would focus more on Tei Fu Chen than it would on his company.

E. Excel used the Debi Boling case as both the

opportunity and excuse to launch a frontal assault on Sunrider and Tei Fu Chen. In 1989, Sunrider had expanded into Australia, Hong Kong, Korea, Thailand, and Taiwan. The pattern of success Sunrider had experienced during its early years in Utah was being repeated in each of Sunrider's new international markets.

In Chen's homeland of Taiwan, Sunrider sales had exploded. For Chen, the success was especially gratifying. Within months of their ribbon cutting in 1987, Sunrider had become one of Taiwan's largest producers and suppliers of herbal food products. In a country where there's an herb shop on nearly every corner, Sunrider's popularity and broad acceptance was no small accomplishment.

One other key indicator of Sunrider's success in Taiwan was that E. Excel soon followed. In the autumn of 1989, Jau-Fei along with a number of E. Excel distributors scheduled a series of meetings and press conferences throughout Taiwan. Hundreds of Sunrider distributors were invited to the meetings, as were E. Excel distributors, the news media, and anyone else who had an interest in what the parents of Tei Fu and Jau-Fei Chen had to say.

One such meeting was held in Taichung on October 18. The Master of Ceremonies, a former Sunrider distributor, kicked off the meeting. From the outset, he artfully emphasized that the meeting's purpose was not to be critical of Sunrider. The following excerpts are from a transcript of that meeting.

M.C.: In September of last year, I formally stepped into Sunrider. Since then I have devoted my life to Sunrider. I am still devoted to Sunrider and I am sure I am not the only one who has feelings for it. It is possible that many of you, my colleagues, feel the same way I do. We have had a deep love for Sunrider. We expected Sunrider to always be as good as it had been in the past.

Now we have come to E. Excel. We need many more colleagues to develop new and better careers. In accepting a new career, we also want to give our thanks to all of our colleagues at Sunrider. They are the ones who trained us. They cultivated us. They guided us. They have helped us learn in a short period of time how to develop our individual careers in the health food industry.

My colleagues, we do not need to attack one another. The reason we are holding this meeting tonight is to hear honest opinions from those who know both companies best [referring to Chen's parents].

The family of Chen is not an ordinary family. They can affect thousands and tens of thousands of families all over the world. Whatever moves they make, whatever decisions they take can affect each and every one of us. For this reason we cannot stand idly by.

Many people in attendance obviously were tape recording and video taping the meeting. The moderator made a half-hearted request that they stop, coupled with a foreboding suggestion.

M.C.: Why do I make such a request and ask for your cooperation? Because I do not want either one of these two companies to get unintentionally hurt. I do not expect that anyone will use a recording device or take photos and expose them to the world, to hurt Sunrider and tens of thousands of salespersons of Sunrider. We want to let Mr. Chen Sr. and Mrs. Chen express freely what they want to say from their hearts.

The knives were about to be unsheathed. The moderator again offered duplicitous praise to Sunrider, and the curious Sunrider distributors.

> M.C.: All of our benefits and good names come from Sunrider. When we drink water we should think of its source. Without Sunrider I don't think we could have the universal acceptance we have today in Taiwan—the direct-sales system of health food products. Without Sunrider, I believe it would not be possible today to have such rapid growth for E. Excel. . . . Before we begin our formal program this evening, I ask all of our colleagues at E. Excel to express thanks for Sunrider. Let us use our applause to express our gratitude.

Applause followed but the stage was already set. The well-orchestrated attack on Tei Fu Chen was about to begin in Taiwan. The program was divided into two parts. During the first half, Papa and Mama Chen were invited to make comments. During the second half of the program they were to respond to questions from the audience. Yung-Yeuan Chen was introduced. He appeared very uncomfortable with his assigned role.

> Papa Chen: Thanks to all of you. You spend your most precious time to attend this meeting this evening. I hope that both sides can grow . . . Every career . . . tonight, my

friends here tonight . . . I am most grateful to you, therefore, I want to say thanks to all of you.

That was Yung-Yeuan's speech in its entirety. The moderator was apologetic.

M.C.: Mr. Chen Sr. has told me that he has never appeared before an audience like this before. He really does not know what he wants to say. He has mixed feelings. Before I turn the time over to you all to let your questions be asked, let's give another round of applause to Mrs. Chen.

Tei Fu's mother was a little more articulate than his father had been and basked in her moment in the spotlight:

Mama Chen: I am most grateful that you have devoted your precious time to attend this meeting. I feel I am very much honored. I only hope that you will assist Sunrider and E. Excel to manufacture health products which can benefit society. This is what we all expect.

The moderator then opened the meeting for questions from the audience. Before one could be asked, he defined the options for his audience to consider.

M.C.: We want to get a truly honest and fair opinion from the investor of these two companies, the true owner of these companies, to speak to us. What he says is most truthful. On one side is the son. On the other side is his daughter. Whatever your conclusion is, bury it in your hearts. And after you leave here tonight, let's not attack one another. After this, I'm sure you will make the best choice.

Let me ask the first question. Please, let me ask if Mr. Tei Fu Chen is your only son? Mr. Tei Fu Chen is the heir to carry on your family name? Sunrider grows up to this state because you have cultivated it for eight years? Now why have you forsaken Mr. Tei Fu Chen, why have you forsaken Sunrider?

As with most of his answers, Yung-Yeuan Chen appeared puzzled and somewhat taken aback by the question.

Papa Chen: Sunrider and E. Excel are both financed by me. Everything in Sunrider is invested by me . . . from his childhood up to his adulthood up to this day, everything is done by me.

The moderator recognized the lack of clarity in Papa Chen's responses. Throughout the meeting he craftily restated or elaborated on every one of the older man's answers—more than twenty times.

M.C.: What he means to say is that he will never give up on his only son because he wants his son to make better products—to make Sunrider become better and better. This is what Mr. Chen meant to say.

A member of the audience asked the obvious question: "Why does the family of Chen create two brands, Sunrider and E. Excel?"

Papa Chen: This is why Sunrider . . . products . . . what E. Excel makes are different. Its formulations are different . . . I cannot say more.

M.C.: I believe what Mr. Chen is saying is the products of these two companies are absolutely different. But he has just mentioned he wanted to set up E. Excel to motivate his only son, Mr. Tei Fu Chen, to make his company better, to manufacture better products.

Another question: "Has Mr. Tei Fu Chen really obtained his doctoral degree? Did he get his Ph.D. degree?"

Chen's father had become tired of standing awkwardly on stage, and told the moderator he wanted to sit down while he responded.

Papa Chen: The situation is this. Whatever it is, he himself knows. I don't have anything to say. In the United States, I cannot read English. I see the paper but it is just white paper with black print.

The moderator seized the moment. He brandished a fistful of papers and turned melodramatic.

M.C.: Maybe it is better for me to answer. (A pregnant pause for effect.) *In my hand is a document* from the U.S. District Court in the state of Arizona. In March 1989, a lady by the name of Boling filed a lawsuit against Sunrider and its owner, Mr. Tei Fu Chen. In this document are the complaints and the answers to the complaints. We have made copies of the answers. My friends, maybe a lot of friends may

misunderstand whether these are attacks. But they are not
attacks. If you have an opportunity to go to the United
States, you can spend $15 to buy a copy of the same docu-
ments from the U.S. District Court in the state of Arizona.
We have already translated and condensed the original text
into Chinese. Let me explain this report to you. And
remember, the United States of America is a democratic
country.

In this document, every time one says something, he
must speak truthfully. If he does not speak truthfully it will
affect his whole life and can be a big blow to him . . . Let me
report here that the plaintiff, Mrs. Boling, asks the question
'Is Tei Fu Chen a medical doctor . . . ?'

The moderator then described fourteen instances in
which Tei Fu Chen's credentials had been challenged by
Boling's attorneys during their deposition of him. Was Chen
a medical doctor, a registered pharmacist, a biochemist, a
senior researcher, a Chinese herbalist? Was the grandfather of
Tei Fu Chen a famous and much-respected medical doctor?
Did he pass on to Tei Fu the traditional knowledge to formulate Sunrider products? Was Tei Fu a national champion
of the martial arts? When Tei Fu was a child, was he weak
and sickly? Was the photograph taken in the office of Tei Fu
Chen with his six-year-old daughter who had used her hand
to break through six layers of thick wood a genuine photograph? The charade had degenerated to a ridiculous level.

The moderator spent much of the rest of the meeting
using Chen's deposition as the weapon with which to attack
Chen's credentials, and his integrity. He repeated for the
fourth time:

M.C.: We spent $15 to purchase this document from the U.S. Court. Anybody can go and get a copy. In the USA it is a public record. After we got the document, we decided it was too long so we condensed it. But anyone can get this information easily. I can guarantee all of this information was the testimony of Mr. Tei Fu Chen at the court.

The meeting was again opened to questions from the audience. "Do Sunrider and E. Excel have the same source for their ingredients?" someone asked. By now, Tei Fu's father apparently was tired of having questions posed to him for which he had no answers. He whispered to the moderator.

M.C.: Mr. Chen said with regard to E. Excel, you may ask Jau-Fei. He does not like to answer for E. Excel. Let Jau-Fei answer for herself.

Throughout the meeting Jau-Fei, although present, had been noticeably silent.

The questions from the audience about Sunrider continued and became increasingly outlandish. Did Sunrider have a problem with salmonella in its products? Didn't Jau-Fei warn her brother of the salmonella problems? Were products contaminated with salmonella destroyed or were they actually brought into Taiwan to sell? To many of the Sunrider distributors in the audience, the questions appeared to have been prepared well in advance. The whole thing smelled.

One question proved to be especially hurtful. "It is said

Mrs. Tei Fu Chen suffers from cancer, is that true?" The
M.C. was quick to respond:

> <u>M.C.</u>: "May I answer this question? *It is true.* This is not
> because I say so but because Mrs. Tei Fu Chen says so. From
> her mouth she told me so . . .

A follow-up question: "Then if she has cancer, is the
cancer related to Sunrider products?"

> <u>M.C.</u>: Nobody can answer this question. Nobody knows
> why people get cancer . . .

The meeting continued for another twenty minutes.
The questions and the purpose of the meeting obviously
were staged to cast Sunrider in the most negative light possible.

It was finally time to bring the session to a close.

> <u>M.C.</u>: "Good night to every one of you. I think we have
> answered a lot of questions tonight. Some of our friends
> may not feel satisfied with the answers, because Mr. Chen Sr.
> and Mrs. Chen, their answers appeared to be superficial. But
> I ask for your understanding. If you were in their position,
> do you dare in the presence of so many people to speak
> about the faults of your own son. He demands that Sunrider
> has to do much better. That's why he organized a new com-
> pany. Each one of us will just have to judge for ourselves.
> Mr. Chen, I do not believe, would like to appear in a place
> like this and attack Sunrider . . . attack his son. In fact E. Excel

and all E. Excel representatives, as I understand it, insist on just one principle—if anything is mentioned it has to have a true fact to be based upon.

The moderator could not resist just one more chance to read from the Boling summary.

> <u>M.C.</u>: What I have in my hand is a document which is a summary of the questions and answers from the lawsuit in the Arizona court. I have such a document. Do you want to understand it? Do you want me to read it? All right, let me read it rapidly. Please listen carefully . . .

The smear campaign against Tei Fu and his company was to be continued at many meetings organized by E. Excel, and through widespread distribution of letters and tapes attributed to Tei Fu's father. Press conferences were convened. The news media willingly covered the story of the family feud and the prodigal son. One magazine story ran the headline "American Food 'Sunrider' Kills People." Obviously there was absolutely no basis in fact.

The themes of the attacks more often were consistent with the defamatory allegations in the Debi Boling lawsuit. The transcripts of Tei Fu's depositions in the Boling litigation supposedly established credibility, even though the case had not yet been heard by the court and despite the fact that Sunrider had not yet been given its chance to be heard.

If the public assault was vicious, the private machinations and rumors were even more egregious. The attack on Chen's integrity was nothing short of character assassination. It was designed to be hurtful to Tei Fu, to Sunrider, and even more particularly to his wife. It was not uncommon for Oi-Lin to receive anonymous telephone calls in the middle of the night when her husband was traveling, and to have the caller ask, "Do you want me to tell you where your husband is tonight?" A long moment of silence would be followed by the telephone dial tone.

CHAPTER SIXTEEN

Rising
to the
Challenge

It is said that you can count the seeds in an apple but not the apples in a seed. As a result of the many seeds of distrust and controversy that had been spread by Sunrider's enemies, all Sunriders suffered the bitter fruit of negative public perception.

During the 1988-89 period, the Chens devoted vast amounts of resources to battle the negative images created by the KSL series, the Utah Department of Agriculture investigations, the Debi Boling lawsuit, and the E. Excel attacks. In the U.S. and abroad, dozens of news reports appeared, trumpeting the negative. If someone was willing to say it, someone in the media was willing to cover it. That was particularly true if the source of the allegations was a member of one's own family.

However, the public relations cloudburst on Sunrider during some of its most important formative stages remarkably also inspired periods of Sunrider's greatest growth. The rain did wash away some distributors, which was to be expected. But most were not dissuaded by rumors and reports that they knew were either half-truths . . . or out-and-out lies.

Most young companies would have crumbled under such intense and ongoing pressure. But the Chens, along with their distributors, dug in their heels and simply worked harder. If quality was to be an issue, then they would build the world's most sophisticated, state-of-the-art herbal product manufacturing complex. If a soy-based product was vulnerable to contamination, then Chen would develop a better product. Nutrien became NuPlus. If the market in Utah declined, then new markets would be cultivated.

The Chens weren't afraid to acknowledge their mistakes. There was no resistance to change whenever they saw opportunities for improvement. They were not hesitant to stand up in front of their "armies of distributors" and deal with truth.

The people that the Chens truly cared about were their *distributors*! If Sunrider could maintain their focus, and keep their customers happy, the Chens believed they could withstand even the most violent storm.

The period from 1988 through 1989 proved to be one of the most difficult in Sunrider's history. But it was a period that marked some of the most dramatic growth, in the company character and in sales. In 1989, sales volume *doubled*, from about $100 million the previous year to $200 million a year.

❧

Ironically, the KSL series broadcast in 1988 led Sunrider to both Richard Richards and me in 1989.

I had heard Dick's name many times while I had lived and worked in Washington, D.C., but I had never personally met him. As one of a small circle of Utahns whose careers had been elevated to the national stage, Dick had an excellent reputation in Utah and in the nation's capital. A native Utahn, Dick had built a successful law practice in the state, and in the mid-'60s became chief of staff for a Utah congressman. That led to his appointment as state chairman of the Utah Republican Party, which opened the door for Dick to become a key operative in Ronald Reagan's presidential campaign in 1976.

When Reagan was elected President of the United States in 1980, he chose Richard Richards to chair the Republican National Committee from 1981 through 1983. By 1989, when Sunrider first contacted him, Dick had a government affairs law practice in Washington, D.C., but was planning to return to Utah for at least a partial retirement. The Chens had other plans in mind.

I too had spent several years in Washington, D.C., as chief of staff to a Nevada congressman and manager of his re-election campaigns. I dealt with the news media almost daily. When we were unsuccessful in a U.S. Senate bid in 1982, I returned to Utah as communications vice president for a large corporate conglomerate. One of the companies they owned was a coal mining company which employed about 2,000 people and mined about six million tons of coal a year in central Utah, making it the largest coal mining operation west of the Mississippi River.

In December 1984, while Utah's Sunriders were celebrating a white Christmas and a BYU national football championship at the Holiday Bowl, I was faced with one of the greatest personal and professional challenges of my life. Less than a week before Christmas, a fire began deep in one of the company's coal mines. While several hundred miners evacuated safely, twenty-six men and one woman were trapped nearly a mile inside the Wilberg Mine. For days, rescuers attempted to reach the coal miners. All were found dead. Before their bodies could be removed, the fire became so intense that rescuers had to retreat and the mine was sealed closed with the bodies inside for nearly a year.

Through the Wilberg Mine experience, I had dealt with

dozens of news reporters and had been interviewed for hundreds of stories. In 1986, I established my own public relations firm which was later merged with a Nevada advertising agency.

Marv Peterson, the highly successful Sunrider distributor, had known Dick Richards for years, but only knew of me because I had been on TV on a regular basis for several months during the mine crisis.

Given Sunrider's media and government relations problems as a result of the KSL series, Marv Peterson suggested to Dr. Chen that he ought to hire Dick and me to assist the company as consultants.

"What's the name of the public relations man?" Chen asked Marv. "Bob Henrie," Marv repeated. The name sounded familiar to Tei Fu Chen. "I think I know him. I think he used to be my neighbor."

Dr. Chen, Marv Peterson, and I met in Chen's room at the Little America Hotel in Salt Lake City, in May 1989. He asked me to spend two days a month at Sunrider to help plan and design media relations protocols and an ongoing public relations campaign. As I walked out the door of Chen's hotel room, Dick Richards was walking in.

I immediately developed a liking for Dick, as did the Chens. It is hard to find a person (especially an attorney) who is practical, genuine, likable, hard working, and trustworthy. Dick is all those things. He also has a lot of compassion. I've walked with him many times through the Los Angeles airport. Never once has he walked past a charity worker collecting "money for the mission" that he hasn't reached into his pocket and found a dollar or two for the disadvantaged.

My first real exposure to Sunrider came at the 1989 Sunrider Grand Convention in Long Beach, California. The theme was "Touch the Sun." I had been asked by Cynthia Muldrow, Sunrider's general counsel, to attend the convention and be prepared to speak for a few minutes on effective methods of dealing with the news media. I arrived early on a Friday afternoon and was amazed at what I saw. Two thousand people from seven countries had the convention center nearly full. I was met at the front doors by a Sunrider employee named Jeanne Feder and was escorted to the front row to sit next to Dr. Chen. I had been given no name tag, agenda, or direction other than to be prepared to speak for a few minutes.

A Canadian distributor, Louise Bureau, was on stage telling about Sunrider's Auto Fund and showing pictures of the new car which Sunrider had purchased for her. Dr. Chen leaned over to me and asked, "Bob, you want to talk?"

"Whatever you'd like me to do," I said.

Chen quickly instructed me. "Explain how the media works. Tell the people why the news stations only want to talk about the negative. Help them to understand how to deal with the rumors." I asked Chen how much time he wanted me to take.

"Take whatever you want," he responded. I spoke for twenty minutes on some of my experiences in dealing with biased and irresponsible news reporters. I could have spoken for hours.

∾

The negative publicity that centered around the Boling case and E. Excel plagued Sunrider for the first two years of my association with the company. Stories ran primarily in the markets where Sunrider was doing well, including California, Arizona, Utah, Hong Kong, and Taiwan. If a story ran in the United States, it would most assuredly be reproduced and circulated in Sunrider's Asian markets. The themes of the stories were consistent: the salmonella incident, the alleged contamination of the Nutrien product that Debi Boling consumed, the credentials of Tei Fu Chen, and the origins of the formulations used in the Sunrider products.

An article in the local Torrance paper, *The Daily Breeze*, was headlined "Herbal Remedies Cause Major Problems," and covered all the above issues. The Copley News Service reporter who wrote the story never contacted me or anyone at Sunrider before the piece ran. It was written, published, and broadly circulated through a number of Southern California newspapers with no sense of fair play and no apparent interest in researching the facts or listening to any of the positive accomplishments of Sunrider. Distributors contacted me, upset by the stories and asking why we were "doing nothing to respond."

Inside Edition, a nationally syndicated tabloid-news-style television show, was much more direct in its approach. Late one Thursday afternoon in May 1991, a reporter and camera crew from *Inside Edition* converged on Sunrider's Torrance headquarters, uninvited and unannounced, and began videotaping. They attempted to interview an unassuming security guard on camera, asking him, "Why does your company have so many complaints?" They insisted on an interview with Dr. Chen, but he was traveling and unavailable. Finally, they packed their camera equipment and left.

I reached the show's producer later that evening at his California hotel room and told him that Sunrider was anxious to tell its story if basic rules of fairness and professionalism would be observed. I protested vehemently the belligerent and bullying tactics evidenced at the company's headquarters. Interestingly, he said he did not believe they would "need an on-camera interview now" and that they would be returning to New York the next day.

New York was not their next destination, however. It was Salt Lake City. Sharon Farnsworth, one of Sunrider's most senior and accomplished distributors, was contacted at her Utah home by a woman professing to have an interest in health, nutrition, and the Sunrider products. Sharon was invited to the woman's apartment and went there, taking along a companion. A couple there feigned great interest in Sunrider and queried Sharon extensively, asking very pointed and leading questions. Sharon, an extremely polite and friendly person, tried to be responsive. Midway through Sharon's presentation, a reporter and camera crew burst into the family room with cameras rolling. The *Inside Edition* crew had been secretly videotaping everything Sharon had said and demanded that she defend herself and the company. An "ambush interview" is an intimidating experience. Sharon did her best to respond to the same old hobgoblins that had been raised time and time again against the company during the past several years.

On May 9, 1991, the *Inside Edition* story ran. The allegations were not new, but several of the people that appeared on camera came as a surprise—including a former distributor and a former employee who had been terminated. The reporter had been armed with legal documents and internal Sunrider memoranda that were referred to throughout the story.

At the beginning of the segment, *Inside Edition* openly acknowledged on the air that they ran the story because they had been contacted by an individual who spoke negatively about Sunrider. In my discussions with the show's producer, I was told that it was based on "research" that had been provided to *Inside Edition*. The producer, of course, refused to tell me who had provided the research, but he acknowledged it was from someone who "had an ax to grind with Sunrider."

Later, I met with Dr. Chen and Cynthia Muldrow to map out an action plan in response to the *Inside Edition* story. We focused on three things: First, Sunrider distributors needed to have an explanation of the story and why it ran. Second, legal action should be initiated against *Inside Edition*. And third, I was convinced that someone on the inside of Sunrider had provided the "research" to the show's producer. We debated who at Sunrider it could possibly be.

Near the end of 1991, the Boling case was finally scheduled for trial. Dr. Chen was shocked to learn that his father would be among the first to testify. Sunrider's legal defense was well prepared. Dr. Donald Kunkel, medical director of the Samaritan Regional Poison Center, told the jury that the thallium found in the sample of Nutrien could not have been in the product when Boling allegedly used it in 1987. "She should have been dead," Kunkel testified. "My feeling is there was no thallium intoxication." In his testimony, Kunkel pointed out that the ingredients for Nutrien were mixed in large vats containing enough material for 300 canisters of the product. If Debi Boling's Nutrien was tainted by thallium, all 300 canisters would have contained the poison, he testified. "There were no reports of mass poisonings from thallium in the United States in 1987," Kunkel testified. In fact, thallium had been banned in the U.S. since 1965. The Boling case was the only incident of alleged thallium contamination that Dr. Kunkel could ever recall.

Ignoring the evidence (or lack thereof), the jury returned a guilty verdict against Sunrider. The testimony of Chen's father proved decisive, although his testimony had nothing to do with Debi Boling or contaminated Nutrien. Jurors simply could not understand why a father would turn against his son—unless the son was indeed guilty of something.

Tei Fu Chen was prepared to testify on Sunrider's behalf, but once he learned of his father's testimony, he had no stomach for any further public spectacle in which father would be pitted against son.

Even though the jury ruled in favor of Boling, they clearly had reservations about her story. She was awarded only a small fraction of the money she had originally sought, barely enough to cover legal expenses. Sunrider lawyers immediately announced plans to appeal the judgment.

The producers of *Inside Edition* seized the opportunity to broadcast yet another story against Sunrider. The previous allegations were repeated. But this time Debi Boling was featured as Sunrider's chief accuser. If Boling didn't get the financial windfall she had sought, she could at least lay claim to her "fifteen minutes of fame." Boling told *Inside Edition* that "I will do whatever it takes to get the attention that I think this company needs. Dr. Chen is not who he says he is. Sunrider is not what they say they are. And their products definitely are not what they say they are."

Inside Edition host Bill O'Reilly closed the segment. "Well, Sunrider says they will appeal that decision and we will keep you posted on the case. Coming next . . . "

CHAPTER SEVENTEEN

Full
Circle

$\mathcal{J}$t would take another year and a half, but the final chapter of *Debi Boling vs. Sunrider* would be written. Ken Andrews, now Boling's former husband, contacted the attorneys in Arizona who had represented Sunrider in the Boling lawsuit. Andrews wanted to come clean.

The setting now was the law office of Lewis & Roca in Phoenix, Arizona. Present were Ken Andrews, five attorneys, and one stenographer. There were no TV cameras. The purpose of the meeting was to take Ken Andrews' sworn testimony—not to generate news headlines. Andrews was appearing voluntarily. He did not seek compensation nor was he compensated for what he was about to say. He was put under oath.

Skip Acuff, with Lewis & Roca, confirmed the purpose of the meeting.

> Acuff: As we see it, the primary purpose of the meeting is to obtain truthful testimony which may lead to independent corroboration of exactly what happened in connection with the participants in the *Boling* litigation, the *E. Excel* litigation, and related matters.

For the next two days, Andrews proceeded to tell a story that is nothing short of astounding. All of the attorneys present believed he was telling the truth. He had with him hundreds of documents that apparently supported every detail of the disclosures he was making. Also he had secretly tape-recorded hundreds of conversations he had participated in that dealt with Boling, E. Excel, and Sunrider.

He provided the attorneys with copies of the relevant tapes and documents.

To recap the case: In February 1988, Debi Boling had filed a lawsuit against Sunrider and its founder, Tei Fu Chen, alleging hair loss, tooth discoloration, and flu-like symptoms—all claimed to have resulted from her consumption of Sunrider herbal food products during the summer of 1987. During the pretrial stages of the litigation, Boling produced two samples of what she claimed was the very same Nutrien product she had consumed. The first sample of Sunrider Nutrien, which she produced almost two years after filing suit, was chemically tested and found to contain 5 percent lead by weight. Almost a year later, in October 1990, she produced a second sample of Nutrien, again which she claimed to have consumed in 1987. The second sample was tested and found to contain nearly 3 percent lead and 3 percent thallium.

Andrews explained how the product came to be contaminated. After the lawsuit had been filed, Andrews studied different herbs to determine what could cause the symptoms that Debi Boling alleged. Andrews' research of herbs failed to find any that could cause hair loss. So he proceeded to "make sure that the product did test for lead, thinking that this would be the ultimate smoking gun." Andrews somehow had come across an internal memo from one Sunrider attorney to another, in which an expert had advised the company that "If lead is found in the product, it would basically make the plaintiff's case."

According to Andrews, in 1989 Mel McDonald,

Boling's attorney, gave Andrews the canister of Nutrien. "When he [McDonald] handed it to me he said, 'If this product doesn't contain any lead then your case is pretty well dead.'" Believing that lead could cause hair loss, Andrews secretly had a lab test the Sunrider product which "came up clean," meaning it contained no lead contamination. Then, according to his testimony, Andrews subsequently "added approximately one-half cup of lead acetate" which he had ground up into a powder to make sure that there were no "hot spots" in the Nutrien.

The problem was that Andrews had put too much lead acetate into the Nutrien container. Sunrider's expert witnesses were prepared to testify that with such high levels of lead, the Nutrien would have killed Debi Boling—not just injured her.

According to Andrews, attorney Mel McDonald was not pleased. McDonald, Andrews, and Boling met at McDonald's office. Referring to McDonald, Andrews testified: "He asked me at that time if I had flunked chemistry. The lead content was exorbitant, way too high, and it was like, gee, if it only would have been half that it would have been real believable."

Andrews worried about the lead evidence being introduced in court. He had never expected the case actually to go to trial. "All along, I thought after the lead appeared, that that would pretty well end the case. They [Sunrider] would be seeking a settlement to get out."

In fact, Sunrider was fully prepared to go to court. Not only were its experts prepared to testify that the level of lead contamination would have killed Debi Boling, but lead does *not* cause hair loss. That presented a new problem for Andrews, but one he set out to solve.

Through a former secretary, Andrews improbably "discovered" a second canister of Nutrien, and saw a fresh opportunity. He contacted McDonald. "He asked me whether I thought it was the same product and I told him I thought it was," testified Andrews. "He asked me if I thought we should go ahead and have it tested. Kind of on the sly-like. 'Well, do you think this one's going to show anything the other didn't?' I said I think it would be highly advisable to test this. This is probably one of those products that you'd really like to test . . . "

The Arizona attorneys asked Andrews if he had added lead to the second canister of Nutrien. "Yes, same exact lead."

How much? "Half."

Now it was at a level that would poison but not kill. How did the thallium get introduced into this sample? the attorneys asked. Andrews smiled and responded, "Very carefully."

Sunrider's attorneys were incredulous. Ken Andrews had just admitted that he contaminated the first sample of Nutrien with lead acetate and then contaminated the second sample with lead acetate and thallium. But there was to be much more to Andrews' testimony.

Andrews' admissions that he had contaminated the two canisters of Nutrien were shocking enough. He also admitted forging an anonymous "honest employee" letter to the presiding judge on the case. Sunrider had filed a motion seeking partial summary judgment at a hearing on

March 30, 1990. Judge William Copple indicated he was inclined to grant Sunrider's motion. Three days later, Judge Copple received a letter written on what appeared to be Sunrider's letterhead. The anonymous letter stated that the writer had heard that Tei Fu Chen claimed that Judge Copple was "in his pocket." The letter concluded that it is "horrible to think . . . that justice can be bought."

Admitting to the product contamination and the forgery of the letter created the possibility that Andrews could be criminally prosecuted. He was well aware of the significance of his confessions. Still, he continued. Four other disclosures were made by Andrews. Each admission, while not necessarily criminal, was equally shocking. If true, each was one more piece of a puzzle that, when completed, painted a picture of conspiracy against Sunrider that coincided neatly with the creation of E. Excel.

Andrews admitted receiving hundreds of stolen Sunrider files and documents that were used in the Boling case. Most were "original documents," including legal files, financial records, and confidential memos written by Sunrider's lawyers. Andrews testified that during the 1989-90 time frame, whenever he needed intelligence on Sunrider, he would typically call a man named Mickey Cochran who was associated with E. Excel. When Andrews requested information, usually within a few days, a plain envelope would arrive containing the information.

Mickey Cochran earlier had been fingered by Jau-Fei Chen and associates as merely Jau-Fei's "religion teacher" who had led her astray in the rubber gloves case, in which she was indicted for criminal fraud [see Chapter Fourteen].

After Cochran and E. Excel had a falling out as a result of the mislabeled rubber gloves, Andrews' primary contact with E. Excel became E. Excel's attorney, Stephen Hard. According to Andrews, Hard "initiated up to 150 calls" to Andrews in the early '90s. Andrews believed Hard wanted "to find out if I could get those Mickey Cochran tapes." Andrews said Hard apparently was concerned that the tapes could implicate E. Excel in the loop of stolen Sunrider documents. Andrews had something that Hard wanted. In return, Hard told Andrews that he was willing to "deliver Chen's father" to testify at the Boling trial.

Two important questions remained. First, how did Andrews initially come into contact with Cochran in 1988? Second, who was the mole inside Sunrider? Taken in order:

> <u>Ken Andrews</u>: I heard about Mickey Cochran from [KSL television reporter] Con Psarras. Did you play that tape last night, where Con Psarras rolls Cochran over to me? Everything started out with Psarras. I flew up to Utah to meet with him. I asked Psarras, I said, well, I need some people to get us some information . . . and he says, well there's a guy that keeps calling me.

Andrews had tape-recorded his discussions with Psarras.

> <u>Ken Andrews</u>: Then he [Psarras] says, here's that guy for you down in Provo or wherever the hell they are out there. And he gives me his [Cochran's] phone number and his name and he [Psarras] says he seems to be supplying me with quite a bit of information.

And who was the mole inside Sunrider, who was apparently mailing or faxing Andrews the information he needed in the *Boling vs. Sunrider* litigation?

> Ken Andrews: It's the one [the tape] where I'm talking to Mickey Cochran and I say, are you sure it's Jau-Hwa that's your inside source? [Cochran responds] Oh yeah, yeah, she's coming to work for us up here.

The pieces of the puzzle at last fell into place. The criminal conduct in the "rubber gloves case" had been blamed on Mickey Cochran, who had been positioned by Jau-Fei simply as a religious instructor and advisor. The Boling case, in large part made possible through the theft of Sunrider documents, had been orchestrated on E. Excel's behalf by Cochran using Jau-Hwa, Tei Fu's sister and Sunrider's controller. The attacks from Chen's parents in the meetings throughout Taiwan had cited the Boling case. The cornerstones of the deceitful Boling suit were the contamination of the Nutrien by Andrews and the testimony of Chen's father. Papa Chen was made available to testify at Debi Boling's trial, in exchange for Andrews delivering information on Mickey Cochran to E. Excel. It had all come full circle.

It is said that politics makes for strange bedfellows. So does the world of business and big money.

In 1993, Sunrider filed a motion to set aside the Boling judgment because the judgment and the settlement agreement had been fraudulently obtained. Sunrider respectfully requested the court to schedule a public hearing on the matter. After several months of deliberation, however, the judge inexplicably elected not to reopen the case. Sunrider distributed a press release detailing Andrews' confession and the fraud that had been perpetuated upon the company. No one in the media was interested in covering the story, not even *Inside Edition*.

Tei Fu and Oi-Lin Chen were dumbfounded. The American system of justice was horribly out of balance. The attorneys and the news media can be used to steal a man's reputation. Rarely do they seem willing to come forward and help restore it.

CHAPTER EIGHTEEN

A
Place
in the
Sun

The adversity and tribulations that Sunrider faced during the company's first eight years easily could have dashed the dreams of the founders and destroyed the business pursuits of the Chens as well as those of Sunrider's independent distributors. Instead, the times of greatest adversity also sparked the periods of Sunrider's most rapid growth and highest achievement. Rather than being ruinous, the calamities were more like intense thunderstorms that caused some damage but also served to cleanse and nourish. "We are not quitters," Chen would say. "Cut off my leg and I'll learn to crawl. Sometimes we move slowly. Sometimes we move faster. But we're always moving forward."

The move to California was to mark a new era for the Chens, their legions of distributors, and for Sunrider. The golden sun of Southern California nourished and strengthened the company and provided a richer soil from which Sunrider could continue its phenomenal growth. Certainly there would be new challenges to be faced, even more ravaging storms to be endured; but in Southern California the sun shines brightly most of the time.

❧

In July 1987, the mayor of Torrance, California, Katy Geisart, stood alongside the Chens at the ribbon cutting of the company's magnificent new headquarters on Lomita Boulevard.

It had been less than three years since Sunrider had held the grand opening for its first corporate headquarters in Orem, Utah. The stark contrast between the Orem building and the new California complex made a powerful statement about how remarkably far the company had come in such a short period of time.

Mrs. Chen had managed the construction of the new building and was justifiably proud with the project's completion. Mayor Geisart was thrilled at the prospect of new jobs and a broader tax base. Tei Fu Chen was just plain *excited*. Dr. Chen had the endearing habit of beginning and ending every speech with the words "I'm so excited!" Anyone who ever heard him say it knew that he genuinely meant it. He was naturally enthusiastic and his enthusiasm was contagious.

Two months later, a similar ribbon cutting opened Sunrider's offices in Calgary, Canada. Chi Chi and Schola Tsai, longtime Sunrider employees, were responsible for the launch and operations of the Canadian facilities. As in the U.S., sales in Canada had skyrocketed and the many outstanding Canadian leaders who had emerged appreciated the Chen's investment in their homeland.

In the summer of 1988, the Sunrider Convention was held in Universal City, California with the theme, "A Miracle to Be Shared." It was a miracle that was increasingly being shared on a global basis. By the end of 1989, Sunrider had operations in the United States, Canada, Hong Kong, Taiwan, Australia, Korea, and Thailand. Malaysia and New Zealand were soon to open.

Sunrider's international success could not obscure the fact that the company was also experiencing bitter challenges. Both professionally and personally, the darkest days in the lives of Tei Fu and Oi-Lin Chen were just ahead.

∾

Darkness fell early on a December evening as Christmas approached in 1989. Tei Fu Chen sat behind a large black desk in his spacious, meticulously decorated office at Sunrider's new headquarters on Lomita Boulevard. He had been on the telephone for several hours with Sunrider leaders in Taiwan, attempting long-distance damage control from his parents' "scorch and burn" campaign against him throughout that nation. The tapes, letters, and press conferences had so emotionally overwhelmed him that there was little else he could think about. But even greater than the burden of his parents' attacks was a much heavier burden anchored to his heart. One part of what was being wildly rumored by E. Excel distributors throughout Taiwan did have an element of truth: Oi-Lin Chen was seriously ill.

A lump that she had discovered in her neck earlier in the year had never gone away. Believing it was just an infection, she nevertheless had a needle biopsy performed, and the doctor concluded that the lump was not cancerous. But as the growth became bigger and bigger, the doctors decided that it needed to be surgically removed and biopsied.

Chen hurried from his office. The hospital was just a short distance away on the same street as Sunrider's headquarters. He was anxious to see his wife and concerned about the surgical procedure. He feared what the results might be.

As he walked down the hall, Chen noticed the lights still on in his sister's office. Like her brother, Jau-Hwa was a hard worker who had devoted her professional life to the company since Sunrider's founding in 1982. Chen often left his office late at night, long after most Sunrider employees had gone home for the day. It was not uncommon to see his sister working well into the evening also.

Alone in her office, Jau-Hwa was dealing with a deep personal conflict of her own. She was torn between her brother, for whom she had worked for nearly seven years, and her parents and sister, Jau-Fei, who had their own use for Jau-Hwa. She was on the inside of Sunrider. She could secretly provide them with a great deal of valuable information.

Tei Fu had always been very sympathetic to Jau-Hwa's relationship with their parents. "Jau-Hwa was always the good girl," he remembers. "Jau-Hwa was the diligent daughter. The hardest working of all of my sisters, the one who worked especially hard to earn the approval of our parents. But it was Jau-Fei, not Jau-Hwa, who my parents favored. Jau-Fei was the 'special one,' Jau-Hwa was not. She has lived her life in Jau-Fei's shadow. That has made her lose her confidence and self-esteem. It's hard to be second best."

Jau-Hwa's marriage to Taig Stewart in September 1989 disappointed Papa and Mama Chen. Taig was Caucasian and relied upon Sunrider for his employment. He drove a Porsche but "always wanted to borrow money," Chen said. "My parents refused to attend Jau-Hwa's wedding. There was not even a reception." Chen believed that Jau-Hwa was devoted to him. He trusted her implicitly. She was the company controller and had access to Chen's most personal files and Sunrider's most proprietary documents. There was no office at Sunrider to which Jau-Hwa did not have access.

Daughters will do strange things for want of a mother's love. Although Jau-Hwa outwardly had declared loyalty to her brother, if Ken Andrews is to be believed, in 1989 and into 1990, Jau-Hwa was in fact spying for E. Excel and for Debi Boling's husband, Andrews. According to Andrews' testimony to attorneys in Arizona, Mickey Cochran had been emphatic in confirming that Jau-Hwa was his "inside source," feeding him sensitive Sunrider documents and planning to desert Sunrider for E. Excel. By her own admission, she took hundreds of documents with her when she left Sunrider to join E. Excel.

Tei Fu Chen called his wife from Taiwan in March 1990 to inform her that Jau-Hwa was leaving the company, reaching Oi-Lin in her room at Torrance Memorial Hospital . Oi-Lin could not believe it. "That's impossible," she cried. It was not only possible, it was true.

According to Dr. Chen, Jau-Hwa assured him she was not leaving to go to work for E. Excel. Both Dr. and Mrs. Chen were dubious but polite. An article in Sunrider's April 1990 *SunSpot* newsletter said, "It is with regret that Sunrider announces the departure of Jau-Hwa Chen-Stewart. Her presence will be sorely missed as her work has been instrumental in the success of Sunrider."

Within weeks, Jau-Hwa was in Utah contacting Sunrider's distributors, telling them "Dr. Chen doesn't really like you," and encouraging them to join E. Excel.

∽

Sitting in the waiting room at the hospital, awaiting the results of Oi-Lin's surgery, was a difficult ordeal for Tei Fu and his children. Even when the doctor said the words they could not believe it: the lymph gland tumor which had been removed was cancerous. She had a nasopharyngeal (nasal) cancer that is common among southern Chinese. Oi-Lin was just thirty-nine years old. Her brother, Man-Kwong, had died from the same kind of cancer at thirty-five. "We were all in shock," Chen remembers. "It was as if we had all been kicked in the stomach. The kids and I were so stunned we couldn't even cry. We were all so worried. We looked at her lying on the bed and felt the surgeon's knife cut into our hearts. We had heard about cancer but we didn't know how terrible it really was."

The following months involved a great deal of suffering as Oi-Lin underwent both chemotherapy and radiation treatments. She lost a lot of weight. Her skin became dark, and because of the radiation, she had no appetite and ate little. The membranes in her mouth were destroyed by the radiation. Additional surgery was required to remove veins and tissue in her neck.

Most people never knew how sick Oi-Lin really was. Tei Fu said, "She was very close to death. The doctors gave her only a 10 percent chance of recovery. At home our kids were scared and worried. We prayed often and they held hands with one another for comfort and to show their unity.

"We refused to discuss the possibility of death. I knew

of my wife's determination. She's a woman who has great faith."

Oi-Lin was in and out of the hospital for nearly six months. Little by little, she started to recover. Dr. Chen spent much of his time trying to formulate an herbal solution that could help save her life. Many people with cancer die not directly from the cancer, but because their immune system becomes so weak they are vulnerable to complications such as pneumonia. Chen experimented with herbs he had never worked with before and made phone calls all over the world to explore every possibility. "Ironically, of all the herbs I tested, I eventually discovered that the very best one is a formulation that I had already developed called Alpha 20C. I firmly believe that Alpha 20C is able to nourish and strengthen the immune system."

After one final operation in May 1990, Oi-Lin's cancer at last was in full remission. The doctors, believing her death inevitable, called Oi-Lin's recovery a miracle. "Had I just eaten Alpha 20C, I would have died," says Oi-Lin. "Had I just done chemotherapy or radiation I believe I would have died. It was the combination of both that saved my life. The chemotherapy and radiation killed the cancer but it was the herbs that helped me fight off the infection." Oi-Lin also knew there was a far greater power in her life that enabled her recovery.

"I believe that God still had something for me to do on this earth," she says. "My religion is everything to me. I've learned to put God first in my life and to let him take care of the things over which I have no control."

Tei Fu adds, with great admiration, "There is no one I

know who has greater faith or who is more devoted to her religion than Oi-Lin."

Oi-Lin was back at work just two weeks after leaving the hospital. She returned in a full-time capacity—as the new president of Sunrider. Her leadership had been sorely missed. The 1990 Grand Convention to be held in Long Beach in July was just around the corner. It was themed "Chariot to the Sun" and promised to be Sunrider's biggest convention ever.

Tei Fu typically opened the convention and spoke about new products, the concept of Regeneration, and the wisdom of the ancients. Foremost on the minds of the distributors, however, was not Sunrider products or philosophy, but the condition of Oi-Lin who had not made a public appearance since her cancer ordeal began.

Rumors had been flying, most of them generated and circulated by Sunrider's competitors. Midway into his speech, Dr. Chen abruptly stopped and turned the time over to his wife. The audience hushed as Oi-Lin, still looking thin and frail, walked on stage to the podium. Without a script or note, she delivered a powerful and inspiring message that came straight from her heart. She spoke of health, of challenge, and of overcoming adversity. Her mere presence was a testament of faith and sheer determination. As she finished, the crowd of nearly 3,000 sat reverentially and then erupted into thunderous applause. The master of ceremonies, Will Godfrey, returned to the podium but for several minutes was unable to say a word.

I was seated next to Oi-Lin and leaned over to her and said, "I would much rather be part of an army of a hundred

lambs led by a lion, than a hundred lions led by a lamb."
She smiled and I sensed that there was not a lamb anywhere
to be found in the Long Beach Convention Center. There
certainly was a lion at Sunrider's helm.

"After seeing her give that emotional speech, the distributors were very moved, and saw a lot of hope," says
Don Caster, a friend and Sunrider leader. "She stood there
and said she would overcome the problem. She never said
that Sunrider products had cured her, which I really
respected her for. A lot of people would have been tempted
to stand there and say 'Alpha 20C saved my life' for obvious
business reasons. But people get so hung up on thinking
that we have to have a miracle in our life, I was glad she told
the truth and said it was a combination of everything, of the
medical treatments and the herbs she had eaten."

Tei Fu could not have been happier, or more proud of
his wife. "My shy, thin, and brave wife—who was such a private person she had never had the nerve to stand in front of
a crowd before—made her first speech by standing in front
of nearly 3,000 of us. Wearing a wig, she tearfully told the
story of her ordeal.

"Oi-Lin was still quite frail, and most of the people in
the audience didn't realize just how sick my wife had been.
They knew that she was ill—I don't believe they knew that
she had been knocking at death's door and that she almost
died while in the hospital."

∾

The lives of Tei Fu and Oi-Lin Chen have taught many
lessons to many thousands of people. I have observed that

whenever the Chens or Sunrider have faced adversity, they use a three-pronged strategy to respond. They develop *new products*, they build *new buildings*, and they expand into *new countries*. It is a proactive approach that requires boldness and sacrifice and also reflects a renewal of commitment that has consistently enabled Sunrider to "rise to the next level."

Sunrider moves to Southern California — Lomita Boulevard office, 1987.

Tei Fu and Oi-Lin Chen in their new offices at Lomita headquarters, 1987.

The Chens celebrate the grand opening of the new Sunrider headquarters with dignitaries from around the world—Torrance, California, 1993.

Sunrider International World Headquarters—Abalone Avenue, Torrance, California.

Tei Fu and Oi-Lin Chens' spectacular 28,000 square-foot home, overlooking Los Angeles and the Pacific Ocean.

Customer service representatives handle several million orders per year in the United States alone.

An average of 1,200 orders are shipped daily from this 80,000-square-foot warehouse at Sunrider headquarters.

The Chens open their first California manufacturing facility at 6th Avenue—
City of Industry, California, 1990.

Arnold Schwarzenegger and the Chens kick off the
grand opening of Sunrider's third manufacturing
facility in City of Industry, 1992.

Groundbreaking—third Sunrider manufacturing facility
in Huang Pu, China.

Sunrider's manufacturing complex in Tianjin, China.

Tei Fu Chen personally formulates each Sunrider product, and oversees all aspects of manufacturing and quality control.

Tei Fu Chen gives Arnold Schwarzenegger a personal tour of a quality control lab, 1992.

Sunrider's state-of-the-art manufacturing facilities—these 600- to 3,500-gallon extraction tanks draw out the beneficial essences of herbs.

Concentrated herb liquid is converted to powder in these unique "flo-coaters."

Six-stories high, the Sunrider manufacturing plant in Taichung, Taiwan, houses Southeast Asia's largest spray dry tower.

This Jones Machine takes powdered herbs and fills individual packets, seals them, and inserts them into boxes which are then labeled.

The Chens receive The National Community Kosher Award from the National Council of Young Israel/Star-K, for outstanding leadership in bringing certified Kosher health products to the marketplace, March 1996.

Tei Fu and Oi-Lin Chen
welcome distributors
from around the world
to their botanical gardens
in the mountains of
Taiwan, 1992.

Tei Fu receives Honorary Doctorate
Degree from China Cultural
University, Taiwan, 1990.

Sunrider's botanical gardens, opened in
1998 at the California world headquarters.

A playful Tei Fu and Oi-Lin Chen.

The Sunrider "brand," the upper half of which resembles a heart.

The Chens attending the inauguration of President George Bush, January 1989.

The Chens celebrating their heritage.

Oi-Lin Chen with Eric, Sunny and Jonathan at the Wailing Wall in Israel, 1998.

The Chen family on the Great Wall of China, 1995 (left to right) Wendy, Tei Fu, Jonathan, Oi-Lin, Sunny, Eric, Reuben.

Celebrating Sunrider's success
at the close of an annual
Grand Convention.

The isolated grave of Tei Fu's father,
Yung-Yeuan Chen, February 12, 1927–
December 11, 1995.

Tei Fu and Oi-Lin celebrate
their 20th wedding anniversary, Hong Kong, 1992.

CHAPTER NINETEEN

Climb to the Top

$\mathcal{J}$n the autumn of 1990, Sunrider completed construction of a building that was to be both the cornerstone and foundation of the company's future. More than a headquarters or distribution center, or the manufacturing facilities that would follow, the opening of the new manufacturing complex on Sixth Avenue in California's City of Industry was a true milestone for Sunrider.

The usual pomp and circumstance that accompanied other Sunrider ribbon cuttings was evident. A band played, dignitaries were on hand, and hundreds of Sunrider distributors shared in the occasion. Both Tei Fu and Oi-Lin Chen hosted the event. Dr. Chen welcomed those gathered with his standard "I'm so excited . . . "

A few days earlier Dr. Chen had given me a personal in-depth tour of the facility. He wanted to be sure that I understood its significance. And what I saw and learned got *me* excited.

I was impressed far beyond expectation. When we began, I was curious. When we finished, there was no doubt in my mind that Sunrider manufactures products that have no real competition.

I wish that I could take every skeptical reporter and government official and give them the same tour. Then, before they prejudge Sunrider, perhaps they would base their conclusions on reality, on fact, on substance, rather than on the rumors and allegations of those who have been intent on Sunrider's failure.

Chen first showed me the massive receiving areas where hundreds of varieties of herbs are imported from various parts of the world, sometimes by the ton. He emphasized the importance of using only premium quality herbs that have been harvested at their peak—herbs that have been culled to use only those parts that contain the desired nutrients. "Some herbs, for example, have toxic roots, nutritious stems, and leaves that have no value," he explained. Sunrider would use only the stems.

"It's like eating a watermelon," he laughed, "the heart of the melon is delicious, the seeds have no use, and only pigs eat the rind. If Sunrider was in the watermelon business, we would grow only the best species of melon, take them to market when they were perfectly ripened, and then process only the heart of the melon. Anyone can sell watermelon, only *one* can produce the world's finest melons. And that person would have to be a watermelon expert."

Expertise is equally important in the formulation of Sunrider products. Again, Chen used a simple analogy. "If you want to bake a great loaf of bread," he explained, "you start with superior ingredients. But then you need a great recipe. Recipes take into account all of the ingredients, and how they interact with and complement one another. Finally, you need a great chef."

The tour lasted nearly two hours. We moved from one section of the huge manufacturing plant to another, each area devoted to a step in the process. I watched teams of workers clean the herbs by hand. We moved to the grinding room where a large hammer mill ground the herbs into fine powders, then on to the mixing rooms, where each product was formulated. The extraction area was next. There, the powdered mixes were poured into huge vats, mixed with water, and then very slowly cooked to extract the herbs' nutrients.

"Sunrider uses only purified water," Dr. Chen pointed out, "and the herbs are steeped at relatively low temperatures, not boiled, in order to retain the 'whole-food' synergy of the plant. Towering condensers then evaporate up to 95 percent of the water, leaving thick, rich, herbal liquids that are highly concentrated.

"Many herbal companies just dehydrate common herbs, grind them up and encapsulate them." Chen spoke proudly, "Here we concentrate *all* of our herbal formulations. Most people would never eat enough quantity of an herb for it to have much effect. That's why we concentrate, sometimes as much as seven pounds of herbs to one pound of finished product."

Many Sunrider herbal products are powdered and placed into capsules or envelopes for easy and convenient consumption. We walked into a room the size of a gymnasium which housed six huge stainless steel "flo-coaters" which convert the liquid herb juice into a concentrated powder, while maintaining the synergy of the original whole-food herb.

In the encapsulation area, fully automated machines filled the capsules with exact amounts of the concentrated herbal powder. While thousands of capsules rapidly move through the equipment, each capsule is individually inspected for quality. Another machine fills sterilized bottles—about 35,000 of them every day which are then capped, labeled, and shrink-wrapped to reduce the risk of product tampering.

We left the manufacturing floor and next visited several quality control laboratories. The immaculate labs were filled with sophisticated, hi-tech equipment, the names of which you would have to be a scientist to pronounce. Quality control at Sunrider had clearly become an obsession. The salmonella incident, as well as the Boling lawsuit, had reinforced to the Chens the absolute necessity of creating products whose quality could never again be challenged.

I was introduced to the plant's quality control manager who supervised two microbiologists and an analytical chemist to determine the quality of the incoming raw ingredients. All raw materials, she pointed out, undergo a battery of tests. Once they pass initial inspection, they are subject to further testing throughout the manufacturing, processing, and packaging stages. "Sunrider has always been the leader in the herb food and cosmetic manufacturing industry," she said. In terms of quality control, Sunrider is light years ahead of the competition. For example, while most other large-scale manufacturers use radiation treatments to sterilize their products, Sunrider has gone to extremes to avoid such practices.

"Our manufacturing techniques are superior and more sophisticated so we don't have to use radiation in our process," she explained. "We buy higher quality raw materials so it sets us apart from the very beginning. By not using radiation in our manufacturing, our finished products are both pure and more natural. What we do is probably a more costly technique, but it allows us to produce products at a superior level."

During the tour, Dr. Chen had pointed out another

strict quality control measure of which he was particularly proud. All the floors in the manufacturing area had been specially treated and coated to prevent microbial growth. The floors were all sealed and had no seams, making it difficult if not impossible for contaminants to collect. "The floors are so clean, I wouldn't hesitate to eat off of them," he smiled.

Victor Ecklund, production manager at the City of Industry facility, pointed out other features unique to Sunrider. Victor had previously worked for other well-known national manufacturers. "One of the reasons we are so careful is because we don't use any preservatives in our products. Without preservatives, we have to be extremely clean. Spotless. This is the cleanest facility I've ever worked in."

Quality control measures also include meticulous inspection of the products once they have been manufactured. The quality control manager, along with her team of twenty inspectors, regularly check finished product to make sure that it has been properly encapsulated, bottled, and packaged. "Sunrider goes way beyond the standard testing of products to ensure that what we sell to the public is the best on the market," explained one inspector. "Having the research and development team work so closely with the quality control personnel is vital. If we didn't work together as a team and conduct thorough research and testing, we could get things done a lot faster *and* cheaper. We go way beyond what is required of us by the government. Most other companies simply don't choose to have the same high standards we do. And that's just part of the reason that we can be sure that Sunrider is producing the absolute best products."

At the conclusion of the tour, I sat with Dr. Chen in the personal office that he keeps in the Sixth Avenue building. As a marketing consultant, a standard question I ask my clients is to name the top three or four differences, or unique qualities about their products, that set them apart from all other competitors. "That's easy," Chen answered, and then quickly rattled off an eight-point summary.

"First, the owners of Sunrider, my wife and I, are responsible for all of the research and development of our herbs, *and* our products. Second, we use only the best part of the herbs. Third, I myself am responsible for the development of the formulations for all Sunrider products. Fourth, we concentrate our products. Most other companies do not. Fifth, we set quality control standards that far exceed government regulation. Sixth, all Sunrider products are based upon Sunrider's Philosophy of Regeneration. Seventh, Sunrider both owns and operates all of our manufacturing facilities. That is the only way we can have absolute confidence in the quality of the products. Lastly, my wife and I are both experts in our industry.

"Now tell me," he asked, "if you know of any other company in the world who can make the same claims?"

In Dr. Chen's office was a huge black wall cabinet with perhaps two hundred small individual drawers. Each drawer was labeled with the name of an herb, and its scientific reference. "Is this where you create new recipes, new ideas?" I asked.

"Sometimes here, sometimes at home in my kitchen," was his response.

I then asked Tei Fu Chen a question which he answered with a response I'll always remember. "Do you think there's anyone in the world that knows more about herbs than you do?"

"I'm sure there is," was his frank response. "If you travel throughout Asia, perhaps you could find a herbologist who has more scientific knowledge than me. But more than just being a pharmacist and a scientist, I consider myself to be an artist. An artist who has studied the techniques of the great masters through the history of time, and who then puts others' artwork out of his mind and creates his own."

A few years later when Dr. Chen created a barbecue sauce which he named "Dr. Chen's Secret Sauce," this quote came to mind. Although the sauce was filled with herbs and other natural ingredients and contained no chemicals or preservatives, some distributors were upset that Sunrider was offering a product that contained sugar. Chen was almost defiant in response. "Sunrider offers dozens and dozens of herbal nutritional products. I developed the Secret Sauce as a healthy alternative to common barbecue sauce. My purpose was not so much to create a health food. I developed Secret Sauce mostly because it tastes so good. It's the only Sunrider product to which I have ever attached my name. It was something that I wanted to share with the people. It was just another part of me."

For ten days in February 1992, Sunrider began commemorating its tenth anniversary with an excursion to Asia designed to let their leaders see firsthand the origins of Sun-rider's herbs, and the homelands of Sunrider's founders. The trip was nothing short of a grand adventure.

The days were very busy, but I managed to find some time each day to walk the streets of Taipei or Hong Kong, and experience the smells, the sights, and the sounds.

There were thousands of fish drying on nets strung over sampans, like canopies. Hundreds of boats crowded into the harbors and waterways, just as the streets over-flowed with people, produce, and enough watches and leather goods to supply a nation.

New building was everywhere. Towering modern skyscrapers under construction were shrouded in bamboo scaffolding fifty stories high. There were ducks hanging by the gaggle in the gallows of meat markets. Giant clams and crabs, the likes of which I had never seen, teemed in large red plastic laundry baskets. Orange octopus tentacles were skewered and sold on a stick, like cotton candy.

The trip was packed with highlights, but clearly the most impressive day was spent traveling to Sunrider's botanical gardens in the remote jungles and forests of Taiwan. Highways turned into steep and narrow roads. Cities became small mountain villages. Mountains became lost in thick blankets of warm fog.

The extensive research done at the botanical garden, where the temperature, humidity, and soil condition are ideal for cultivating and researching herbs, was yet another testament of the extraordinary efforts of the Chens in achieving superior quality.

Dr. Chen spent hours leading one group of Sunriders after another through the expansive terraced gardens and greenhouses. His mastery of herbs was most impressive. Much like the personal tours he gives at the manufacturing facilities, Chen leaves no stone unturned. Hundreds of herbs are nurtured, studied, and refined at the botanical gardens. Chen knew every one, like a painter knows the colors on his palette.

The return trip to Taipei was also fascinating. The long caravan of buses meandered down the mountainsides, past the endless quadrants of rice paddies. Women and children were hunched over, nurturing their rice shoots as Chen did with his mountain herbs. A farmer and his plow, powered by a water buffalo, cut uneven furrows, much the way his ancestors did thousands of years ago.

The following day, Sunrider held its first international Leadership Conference in the Orient at the largest meeting facility in all of Taiwan. Over six thousand people attended.

Most had heard or read of the E. Excel attacks on Sunrider. The convention focus was on leadership, loyalty, and longevity.

The Chens celebrated their twentieth wedding anniversary in both Hong Kong and Japan. I watched the couple dance after cutting an anniversary cake given to them by their distributors at a party held in their honor. They danced slowly, closely, and looked into each other's eyes all the while they danced. They seemed oblivious to the crowd that had gathered around them. I stood and curiously watched. There was an obvious bond of love that connected the two. The Chens were different in so many ways, but complemented each other in most. There was balance. There was harmony.

At the convention in Hong Kong, it was Mrs. Chen upon whom the spotlight shined. Here she was in her hometown less than two years after her near-death experience with cancer, standing before a packed crowd in the Hong Kong Coliseum being recognized as one of her country's most accomplished and distinguished women. The only word that came to my mind was *triumph*!

∾

There are very few women in the world who own and serve as hands-on president of a several-hundred-million-dollar international business enterprise.

As president of Sunrider International, Dr. Oi-Lin Chen faced a mountain of responsibilities. By 1992, Sunrider had nearly two hundred employees at its headquarters in Torrance and over three hundred employees working at the manufacturing facilities. Sunrider also had operations managers and staff in Canada, Hong Kong, Australia, Korea, Taiwan, Thailand, Malaysia, and Europe. Plans were underway to open offices in Indonesia, Israel, Japan, and Mexico.

Mrs. Chen's style was a model of efficiency and patience. She dealt with hundreds of issues and dozens of phone calls and meetings every day. At night she would return home to parent the Chens' five children. When the children had finally retired for the evening, both Oi-Lin and Tei Fu would talk to their distributors and managers on the phone, some of whom were halfway across the world. Rarely did the Chens go to bed before midnight.

In her new role as company president, Mrs. Chen viewed herself as more of a student than an executive. She knew she had a great deal of business knowledge yet to learn. But she was also a very quick study. In meetings, she would listen for as long as it took to understand what was necessary for a decision to be made, and then she would move forward aggressively. "There's a time to talk, and a time to act," I heard her say more than once.

She dealt daily with the problems and mistakes of others and was usually quite tolerant. However, she had little time for excuses. One day she voiced her frustration to me concerning a manager who had fouled up, and had taken a great deal of time to explain his mistake to Mrs. Chen. "Hearing a long explanation doesn't help," she vented. "All I needed to hear was 'I'm sorry.'"

Some distributors and employees were skeptical at first. How could a medical doctor with no practical business experience manage a rapidly growing international enterprise? "She came home very upset after meeting with distributors for the first time," Dr. Chen said. "But I believed in her, and not just because I'm her husband. I knew of her ability. The distributors did start to sit up and take notice when she reorganized the way we do business, cut our printing costs, and made it much easier for them to order products. She renegotiated our deal with Paget and saved us a great deal of money.

"Having Oi-Lin as president of Sunrider has been great for everyone. How many people can go to work each day with their wife? I am very fortunate. I always say in my family, that if either Oi-Lin or I should be lost, it should be me. Yes, I create most new products. But Oi-Lin takes care of the family, she runs the business, and she is a much stronger person. She is also very, very smart."

Dr. Chen continued in his role as Sunrider's CEO and spent his time developing new products and overseeing the worldwide manufacturing facilities, the marketing functions, and the legal challenges. Much of his time was spent traveling the world as Sunrider's chief diplomat. Chen would speak of Chinese herbs and philosophy to large crowds, often numbering in the thousands, in city after city, country after country, day after day. He also spent a great deal of time with Sunrider's far-flung distributor leaders, teaching and training. It was typical for him to speak at three or four meetings in a day and then take a small group of leaders out for a two- or three-hour dinner at ten o'clock at night.

Dr. Chen's tireless, pioneering efforts were recognized around the world in academic as well as business circles. Among many other honors, in June 1990 he was awarded an honorary doctorate degree "of extraordinary significance"—the first entrepreneur to be so honored—from Chinese Cultural University, Taiwan. In November 1993, Wuhan University, one of the most respected institutions in China, celebrated its 100th anniversary in part by bestowing the title of "Honorary Professor" on Dr. Chen for his devotion to promoting Chinese culture.

Oi-Lin's health, strength, and appearance improved dramatically in the year following her cancer. Both she and Dr. Chen made the Kandesn product line of skin care and beauty products a top priority. A revamped Kandesn product line called Kandesn 2000 was to be introduced at the 1992 Grand Convention.

Like Sunrider's herbal nutritional products, superior quality was to be the Kandesn standard. Because skin is the largest and most obvious of the body's organs, the Kandesn approach to beauty was to promote healthy skin and a more youthful appearance. Kandesn fit perfectly as part of Sunrider's program of health and nutrition. Just as with the body's other systems, the Sunrider philosophy was to create healthy skin through balance, achieved through proper nourishment and cleansing. The Kandesn 2000 line of products was designed to nourish and cleanse, and would be the only major skin care line developed and manufactured by a food company. With the skin-care, personal-care, and cosmetic industries earning over $30 billion a year in sales, the untapped potential of Kandesn was staggering. Kandesn 2000 could provide thousands of women with an opportunity to work at home, either part-time or full time, in an industry that they would find to be fulfilling and rewarding.

Sunrider Grand Conventions are always the major event of the year for the company. It's the one time of the year when distributors from around the world come together to learn, celebrate, be recognized, and be entertained.

Convention week usually begins on a Monday with leadership training seminars and tours of the manufacturing facilities. Product fairs, Kandesn training, ribbon cuttings at new facilities, and special meetings follow. Near the end of the week the general sessions are held, typically on a Friday and Saturday, followed by a spectacular gala evening of food, entertainment, and dancing on Saturday night.

The 1992 Long Beach Grand Convention was kicked off when film star Arnold Schwarzenegger and over 1,000 distributors participated at the ribbon cutting at Sunrider's recently constructed warehousing and manufacturing facilities in the City of Industry, named Nelson I and Nelson II. The facilities added 435,000 square feet of manufacturing and distribution space, doubling Sunrider's existing capacity and creating over 300 new jobs in Southern California.

Schwarzenegger addressed the crowd.

"Let's just say a few things about the man. He came from a foreign country to the United States. He started out with nothing and made it to the top. He had an idea and a vision and turned his dream into reality. He's admired by millions of people all over the world. But enough about me . . . now let's talk about Dr. Chen!"

By Friday, the general sessions were underway, attended by about 2,500 distributors. Dr. Chen spoke in the morning and talked about the Philosophy of Regeneration, and the potential of "tomorrow's foods" meeting the demands of a world increasingly concerned about health and interested in herbal nutrition.

Dr. Chen introduced several new products, including

an improved nutritional snack called SunBar, in a variety of new flavors—cherry, mango, pineapple, and banana. "I am excited!" he concluded and the crowd thundered their approval with sustained applause.

The unveiling of the Kandesn 2000 line by Mrs. Chen was scheduled for early Friday afternoon. It was to be the first major product presentation that Mrs. Chen had ever made at a Grand Convention. Basically shy in nature, she was understandably nervous.

Shortly before noon, the Chens, Dick Richards, and I were called out of the convention by Sunrider's new general counsel, Ralph Pais. "We have a problem," he said gravely. "A raid is underway at company headquarters by U.S. Customs agents." We hurried back to the Chens' suite at the hotel.

Ralph was on the phone with another attorney at Sunrider's headquarters in Torrance. A busload of about thirty Customs agents, armed and wearing flak jackets, had converged on the corporate offices and the Chens' home in a commando-style raid. They had search warrants to seize volumes of financial and legal files at the headquarters. The agents had herded many of the shocked Sunrider employees into a conference room while their individual offices were searched.

Someone had provided Customs officers with a schematic of the building's floor plan, along with detailed lists of documents and in which offices they could be found.

According to sworn statements of employees who were there, the Customs agent in charge of the search, Stephen DiCiurcio, strutted through the offices, a toothpick hanging from the corner of his mouth, gun in hand. He physically pushed several employees aside, and once pointed his gun in the air at the ceiling as if he were about to fire. According to witness accounts, he also told several people to start looking for new jobs, because "we've caught the big koi fish now."

As details of the search still in progress were conveyed to the Chens, they were both visibly shaken. Just when all the difficulties and heartaches of the past five years seemed to be behind them, a new dark, ominous cloud appeared. It was a cloud that bore a striking resemblance to the storms of years past.

Mrs. Chen was scheduled to be back on stage to make her Kandesn 2000 presentation in less than a half-hour. How could she possibly stand and speak to the large convention crowd and maintain her composure, her focus? I asked if she would like me to find one of the Kandesn leaders who could fill in for her on the program.

"No," she said quietly. "I just need a few minutes alone." She walked into the bedroom and closed the door. Fifteen minutes later the Chens, Ralph, Dick, and I walked back to the convention center. We walked in silence.

For the next two hours I watched Mrs. Chen project herself in a powerful and poignant way. She wore an elegant gown embroidered with images of butterflies, the symbol of Kandesn. Oi-Lin was the personification of a butterfly's metamorphosis. It was hard to believe that only two years earlier she had stood in front of a convention crowd, her color pale, wearing a light dress with a bright rose in her lapel, and a loose wig to cover her baldness. Then, she

spoke in strained, coarse whispers, and only for a few minutes at a time.

Now, in 1992, she radiated a physical beauty, and
much, much more. A video played "The Beauty Within,"
whose lyrics *told* the Kandesn story. Mrs. Chen *projected* the
"beauty within," a story of character, faith, and compassion.
My admiration for Mrs. Chen was elevated that day, as was
my confidence that whatever challenges lay ahead, somehow everything was going to be all right.

The government raids and searches that started in July
1992 at Sunrider's convention continued into 1993. Subsequent searches were to be equally aggressive and confronta-
tional.

During the convention, a search was also conducted at
the Chen's home in Palos Verdes. Wendy Chen, only seventeen years old at the time, was asleep and the only one at
home when agents arrived in the early morning. Upon
answering the door, she was frisked while still in her night-
gown.

Eight months later the agents returned. No resistance
had ever been offered, but the agents still unholstered their
guns and pointed them toward both parents and children.
"Do you have a warrant?" Dr. Chen asked.

"We'll show it to you in due time," was the curt
response.

The agents stayed in the house for nearly eight hours,
during which time no one was allowed to use the bathroom
unless the door was kept open. Every room in the house

was searched. Even the children's computer files were con-
fiscated. The belligerence and intimidation was beyond
comprehension, and was especially traumatic for the Chens'
young children.

In 1993, a second search was conducted at Sunrider
headquarters. Chief agent Stephen DiCiurcio was again in
charge, and employees later testified that aggressive and
hostile tactics were once again used. Employees who asked
simple questions were told to "Shut up and stay out of it."
Upon finding a door locked, an agent told Dr. Chen's secretary that if she didn't get him a key within thirty seconds,
he was going to kick the door down.

While agents rifled through Dr. Chen's rare antique
collection, one Sunrider employee stated that he wanted to
observe the search to make sure that no damage was done
to any of the pieces in the collection. DiCiurcio said to him
in a deadly serious tone, "Do I have to handcuff you and
drag you out of here?"

When the agents appeared ready to pack and remove
the items, another employee expressed concern over the
fragile nature and high value of the antiques. The employee
asked an agent how he intended to remove one of the very
large antique pieces. "We'll chain saw it apart if we have
to," the agent snapped. Randy Crawford, a longtime Sunrider employee, held his ground. He made sure that the
antiques were properly packed and carefully removed.

According to her own later testimony, upon leaving
Sunrider Jau-Hwa Chen had taken with her a great number

of Sunrider files and documents. With her mother's encouragement, she contacted the Internal Revenue Service, as well as other government agencies, alleging that her brother, Tei Fu Chen, had underpaid taxes and customs duties through his business arrangement with Paget, the Hong Kong company owned by members of Oi-Lin's family. Ironically, during the years in question, Jau-Hwa was Sunrider's controller.

Thus began yet another family-driven saga that was to last five years, cost Sunrider tens of millions of dollars, and would forever impact the lives of Tei Fu and Oi-Lin Chen and their Sunrider family.

CHAPTER TWENTY

Dawn
of a
New
Decade

The heights by great men reached and kept
Were not attained by sudden flight,
But they, while their companions slept,
Were toiling upward in the night.

——Henry Wadsworth Longfellow

This quote understandably is a Chen favorite. It personifies Tei Fu and Oi-Lin's own Olympian work ethic, which includes many years of days that rarely have seen them in bed before midnight. While the Chens probably would be the last to claim their personal labors have been pivotal to Sunrider's meteoric rise, those of us close to both them and the company know this is the case. But the Chens have done far more than work hard—they have worked *smart,* and have taught other Sunriders to do the same. Consider, for example, the concept of duplication.

Take a dollar and double it every day for just ten days and you'll have a thousand dollars. It's a simple demonstration of the power of duplication. Take a company worth $330,000 in annual sales and double it every year for ten years and the result is $330 million in sales. After just ten years in business, that is exactly what Sunrider had accomplished. Sales had increased a *thousand-fold* from Sunrider's first year.

Nineteen ninety-three was the dawn of a new decade for Sunrider. Though shadows loomed from the previous year, notably ongoing government raids sparked by Tei Fu's family, the Chens, as always, were determined to stay focused on their central mission of building Sunrider and offering more people in more places the blessings of health and the potential of wealth. To that end, the new year found Dr. Chen and me in Hawaii, sitting Japanese-style on the floor around the dining table in his family's magnificent home at Diamond Head Beach. We had just returned from a two-day leadership conference at the Hyatt Regency Waikoloa on the Big Island. It was late at night and we were snacking from a large bowl of fresh strawberries that Chen dipped in sweetened condensed milk.

I remarked to Chen that, overall, 1992 had been great for Sunrider. The conventions in Taiwan and Hong Kong had been immense successes and the '92 convention at Long Beach had been one of the best I had ever attended.

"What do you think the key to growth is?" Chen asked. Since we had just been talking about it, I said "Duplication."

"Right," he answered. "What's the key to duplication?" I waited for him to answer his own question.

"Simplicity and consistency," he said. "Duplication is impossible without those elements. Tell me what we need to do to achieve greater consistency in Sunrider?" he asked.

It was clear that Dr. Chen had a train of thought he wanted to pursue. I listened. "We need to build leadership," he said. "I'm not talking about leadership from Sunrider. The leadership for Sunrider's second decade must come from the *distributor force!*"

In the few short years that I had been involved with Sunrider, tremendous progress had been made in simplifying the presentation of the company, its products, and philosophies. Simple, easy-to-read one-page "product inserts" had been produced that were written in clear, concise language that actually conveyed something. Flipcharts were designed to tell the Sunrider story in a quick and easy format. We had produced several videos to enable distributors to simplify Sunrider's complexities, including the Philosophy of Regeneration and the concepts of balance and harmony.

Tei Fu and Oi-Lin made it a personal goal for 1993 to "go to the people." Their crowded calendar proved their commitment. After the leadership conference in Hawaii, a convention was held in Japan. Regional training seminars followed in Dallas, Vancouver, and San Francisco, New York, Florida, Toronto. Then it was on to a convention in Hong Kong and grand openings in Indonesia and Mexico.

After the International Grand Convention in Anaheim, California, in July, the Chens attended training seminars in Europe, Taiwan, Korea, Australia, Malaysia, Thailand, Chicago, and Las Vegas.

As the Chens knew well, the challenge of owning and managing a worldwide company could be reduced to one inevitable conclusion: "To achieve success, you not only have to work hard—you have to work smart." It didn't make any difference whether a person was a brand-new distributor, a top-ranking distributor, or the owner of the company, success required hard work and the Chens were resolved that the rewards of Sunrider's success would flow to those who were actively working the business.

For one week in June 1993, it wasn't necessary for Tei Fu and Oi-Lin to take Sunrider to the people—the people were coming to them. Nearly 3,000 distributors traveled to Los Angeles to attend Sunrider's annual Grand Convention, and the ribbon cutting for Sunrider's new World Headquarters. The week began at the Los Angeles International Airport where hundreds of Sunrider distributors and employees carrying welcome banners and waving red and gold flags greeted the arrival of the international distributors. The air of excitement continued through the entire week, ending on a memorable high with country superstar Lee Greenwood singing "God Bless the USA" at the closing ceremonies.

Highlight of the week was the inauguration of Sunrider's stunning new world headquarters on Abalone Avenue. With an array of dignitaries including former California Governor George Deukmejian, and with traditional Chinese kites flying overhead, 3,500 people watched and cheered as the Chens ceremoniously cut a fifty-foot red ribbon to symbolize the official opening of the spectacular $35 million facility that encompassed more than 300,000 square-feet. Baskets of white doves were released. The crowd roared its approval. Echoing the convention theme, it was "A Time to Soar."

For three years, Mrs. Chen had overseen construction of the new building. Dr. Chen called it, "Our greatest production." At the ceremony he stood to thank his wife and distributor family. "I dedicate this building to you. You are the ones who have made *this dream* come true. This marks a new beginning for Sunrider."

The headquarters structure is itself a towering piece of art. The Chinese concept of *feng shui* governed the building design and is intended to situate the building and its contents in a manner where balance and harmony with nature and the environment are achieved. Impressive art work and stunning sculptures enhance the building throughout. None of the workstations face in a westerly direction, because of the association to the setting sun. The entrance doors were set at forty-five degree angles to face the main street, in effect saying that the road to success leads straight to Sunrider. The architecture of the building, like Sunrider itself, blends the best of Eastern tradition with stunningly futuristic design.

Producers of the movie "Armageddon" were allowed by the Chens to use both the interior and exterior of Sunrider headquarters for scenes depicting NASA's space-age headquarters. The Chens' building includes a full-scale gallery illustrating the theme of Harmony, featuring an array of Chinese art and artifacts, and historical exhibits showcasing China's 7,000-year history (including the first 3,500 years of unwritten history), and Tei Fu Chen's beautiful art collection. On the back wall of the gallery is a timeline that explores the dynasties spanning China's history and the art and innovation that represent each period. For more than a decade, Tei Fu has collected art and artifacts from each of the major periods in China's history.

It is not the monetary value of Chen's prizes that impresses me, but the passion and reverence he feels for his art. For Chen, collecting the artifacts wasn't a hobby, and it was far more than an investment. Each artifact has a story to tell. Each reflects the thinking and values of Chinese culture at a given point in time.

Chen loves studying the stories told by each of his art pieces. At heart, Tei Fu Chen *is* an artist and Sunrider is his gallery.

∽

During the 1993 summer convention, Dr. Chen emphasized his four-part strategy previously outlined for his leaders earlier in the year in Hawaii. His goals were straight-forward: keep the existing marketing plan intact, take the company to the people, build a foundation of unity that can withstand outside attack, and move Sunrider products more into the mainstream.

Some distributors frankly disagreed with the direction Chen was taking the company. They pressed hard to restructure the distributor compensation program, referred to as the "marketing plan." Some were longtime distributors who had seen their monthly Sunrider checks shrink as they worked the business less. Others were new distributors who struggled for success and found it easy to blame their disappointing results on Sunrider's marketing plan.

Debate over the marketing plan grew into major divisiveness, especially at Sunrider's Advisory Board meetings. The topic dominated meeting after meeting and the subject became increasingly bitter. Disagreement on the board spread like a cancer through Sunrider's distributor network. For the Chens the contention had created yet another family feud. They became concerned that the greatest threat to Sunrider's future was not from outside attacks but from internal dissension. Unlike the tax case and E. Excel, two thorns over which they had little control, the Chens were determined to end the rift over the marketing plan. A two-day leadership retreat on Catalina Island was held in the fall of 1993. An outside "facilitator" was brought in to conduct the meetings. Everyone had the opportunity to raise any issue they desired, freely expressing their feelings and opinions.

After two days, agreement was reached and the leaders boarded the boat to return to the Long Beach harbor. Proposals to make major modifications to the marketing plan were dead and buried. What had created Sunrider's success from the outset was not a marketing plan—it was focusing on the basics of the business: using the products, selling the products, and finding others who had a desire to do the same.

The debate was over. The overwhelming majority of leaders stood together. Those who couldn't accept the group decision were asked to pursue opportunities elsewhere. A house divided cannot stand.

A few months later, in early 1994, Mrs. Chen announced that Bob and Kay Goshen had purchased the Sunrider business of Robert and Carol Lovell. The Lovells had been part of Sunrider from nearly the beginning, and I along with many others held them in high regard. Robert and Carol had chosen a new path to their future, while Bob and Kay had chosen the Sunrider path to accomplish their goals. In his own inimitable Oklahoma style, and with a broad grin on his face, Goshen looked forward and encouraged his fellow distributors: "The dogs are barkin' . . . and the caravan's a movin' on!"

∾

While some leaders chose to pursue new paths, by and large the Sunrider leadership in the field remained intact. A two-day special training seminar was held for them at Sunrider headquarters in December 1994. The Chens invited about seventy-five of their top North American distributors to attend. These were the leaders that the Chens had consistently relied on through the years to "make things happen" in the field. I had come to know every one of the leaders in this diverse group quite well. Many had been with Sunrider since its founding. To a person, these were some of the most outstanding people I had ever had the privilege of knowing.

"Life is a journey with many paths," Mrs. Chen would say. The leaders who had chosen to journey with Sunrider over the "long path" invariably enjoyed a level of personal fulfillment and financial achievement that they likely would not have realized elsewhere.

As president of Sunrider, Mrs. Chen opened the meeting with an overview of the plans and challenges for the upcoming year. Nineteen ninety-five would prove to be a crossroads for Sunrider.

Dr. Chen talked about his plans for new products. He had developed a "new and improved Vitalite Weight Management line," as well as the new "Oi-Lin Signature" line of Kandesn products. He also envisioned producing a variety of replacement products—snacks, bars, cereals, and beverages that could serve as convenient, tasty, and healthy alternatives to the empty calories of fast food that had become a staple in the lives of most people.

Someone asked why Sunrider was constantly in the process of change. "Of course we change," Mrs. Chen responded. "If we do not change, how can we become better?" But the foundation of the Sunrider business, including the Philosophy of Regeneration and the commitment to superior quality, had never changed—not once in Sunrider's thirteen-year history.

The health consciousness of most Americans was also changing, along with their open-mindedness to "alternative approaches" to health. More and more people were searching for healthier ways to eat well.

Movie stars openly touted their favorite herbal products. The May 1994 issue of *Mademoiselle* magazine featured Sunrider's own Fortune Delight as the drink of choice of supermodel Cindy Crawford. A highly rated PBS series, "Healing and the Mind with Bill Moyers" examined the virtues of the Chinese approach to health and herbs. In a book with the same title, Moyers explained that he went to China as a "skeptic" and returned a "believer."

Even the concepts embodied in the Philosophy of Regeneration were gaining acceptance. A 1993 *Business Week* article featuring America's new interest in herbs reiterated what Dr. Chen had been teaching for years: "What's new is the idea that these potent compounds could offer health benefits *before* people get sick, saving both lives and healthcare dollars."

The health concepts that Sunrider had been promoting for over a decade were rapidly gaining mainstream acceptance. "Think of the potential!" Dr. Chen exhorted his leaders. "Sunrider is the herbal nutritional *leader*. If we can just focus on the basics of who we are, and who we've always been, there is no limit to the heights to which we can soar!"

Following the two days of meetings in December 1994, the Chens, as was their custom, invited their leaders to a lavish Christmas party at their new home. The house was spectacular and had been beautifully decorated for the season. The mood was festive. Everyone sang Christmas carols, and many joined Tei Fu in entertaining the crowd with karaoke performances. As always, the food was superb and included everything from lobster fruit salad to giant boiled prawns with heads still attached. After dinner, everyone danced in the Chens' trendy discotheque located in their home adjacent to a six-car underground parking garage.

The party at the Chens' home served as a not-so-subtle reminder of the "Sunrider lifestyle"—a lifestyle that the Chens wanted each of their leaders to experience, enjoy, and project. It was the *good life*! Good friends, good health, good food, good times. It was all there in rich abundance.

It was appreciated. No one took anything for granted, especially not Tei Fu and Oi-Lin Chen. They remembered all too well what it was like to live in a basement apartment without any heat, and to eat Ramen noodles from an electric fry pan in a cheap motel room.

As the evening concluded, Dr. Chen took one last opportunity to thank his leaders and to encourage them to promote the 1995 Grand Convention in China. Appropriately, the theme the Chens had decided upon was "Capture the Dream."

"Most of you are already reaching *your* goals," he said. "At Sunrider, our mission is to help other people reach *their* goals. In China there are over one billion people. They are very humble. Many are poor. But they are willing to learn. They want a better life, just as you do."

"Travel with Sunrider to China next year," he encouraged. "Get to know our Chinese culture, our tradition, and our determination to make a positive impact on the world. You will appreciate what you have at home. But make the trip not with the expectation of what you'll bring home, but instead with the satisfaction of what you'll *leave behind.*"

As 1994 concluded yet another chapter in Sunrider's history, there was no doubt that the company was on a roll. More than a time to soar—it was a time to soar higher, faster, stronger. The distributor force was energized and working harder and smarter than ever before.

Along with the exodus of several of Sunrider's former top-ranking distributors, the divisiveness and negative attitudes also seemed to fade. New leaders were emerging, and it was refreshing to feel the energy and dynamism of those who were "out among the people."

The efforts of Dr. and Mrs. Chen to focus on building leadership, unity, and loyalty over the previous two and a half years was far more timely than they may have realized. New heights are usually precursors to new lows. Nineteen ninety-five promised to be a year with the potential for both.

CHAPTER TWENTY-ONE

Triumph
and
Tragedy

"What we call the 'American Dream' is a dream of independence and prosperity. This is not only an American dream—it is a worldwide dream. We want to bring this dream to China, to give to our Chinese people."

Mrs. Chen's welcome set the stage for a week not to be forgotten in Sunrider's history. What brought six thousand people together in Beijing, China in 1995 was encompassed under the banner "Capture the Dream."

Dr. Chen had been reluctant to use the word "dream" as part of the convention theme. To Chen, Sunrider's mission dealt with *reality*, not dreaming. Still, he knew that for most Chinese, the pursuit of financial independence, and the hope for a better life, had yet to become a reality.

You could call it a hope, a goal, an aspiration. The semantics meant little to the overflowing masses at the convention. Sunrider had what the world wanted.

Long before the convention, when the Chens first decided to build their business in China, they had resolved they would "do it right." Although Dr. Chen was born in Taiwan, and founded Sunrider in the United States, his heart belonged to China. The Chens would invest vast sums in China, building modern, technologically advanced manufacturing facilities in Tianjin and Guangzhou, with additional facilities in the planning stages.

Sunrider had been a good "corporate citizen" in China, providing relief to victims of earthquake and flood disasters, and funding campaigns to support young artists and fight against drug abuse.

The Chens' efforts had not gone unnoticed. The

Tianjin Economic Technological Development area would later honor Sunrider as one of the "Top 100 Star Enterprises in China," for achievement in advanced technology, high quality control, and scientific management.

The Sunrider standard of superior quality was evident in every detail of the Grand Convention. It was a huge success. Leaders from many countries had heeded Dr. Chen's admonition to focus on "the basics." Speakers at the convention talked about the value of loyalty, positive attitude, and being a "product of the product." Dr. Chen's themes of eat, recruit, and duplicate were repeated often, and by many.

Tei Fu and Oi-Lin jointly conducted the general sessions. Their children often joined them on stage. After Wendy had introduced one of the newest Kandesn products, Mrs. Chen stood alongside her twenty-year-old daughter and shared her own product testimonial: "Sunrider changed my life. Kandesn changed my appearance. I love Kandesn because I can stand next to my daughter, and look like her sister."

It was true!

The convention that enabled thousands to discover China also enabled China to discover Sunrider. At one point, more than 30,000 people were signing up as new Sunrider distributors in China *each month*. The growth was phenomenal, but in a country of more than 1.2 billion people, the surface had barely been scratched.

Media representatives, dignitaries, and various government officials attended the convention, and developed a new understanding and a greater respect for the U.S. company whose philosophies and founders were deeply rooted in China.

Discovering the roots of China was a true once-in-a-lifetime experience for the visiting Sunrider distributors. They walked the vast expanse of the Forbidden City, long held from public view, where emperors and world leaders have lived for over 500 years. They toured the buildings and examined the artifacts that symbolize balance, harmony, and longevity. Everyone paused at Tiananmen Square, the largest public plaza in the world, where history has been made through the centuries.

The highlight of the trip was, of course, to walk along the Great Wall of China. Two centuries before Christ, work began on the great wall. It is an engineering and construction feat that has no rival. Following mountain peaks and valleys, it is 3,700 miles long, and is the only man-made landmark visible to the naked eye from outer space.

To watch thousands of Sunrider distributors of many nationalities, all wearing their Sunrider shirts and jackets, stand atop what may well be the most stunning structure ever built, was a sight that will not be forgotten.

Most remarkable to me was the realization that the Great Wall of China—which stretches for thousands of miles, and which required centuries of labor—is only a very small part of a country whose history spans 7,000 years.

China is a country rich in culture, beauty, and diversity. The wisdom and innovation of a country with such a long and remarkable history had been Tei Fu's lifelong passion, and through Sunrider he was able to share at least a part of it with the world. If the Chinese had the capability to design and construct such a wondrous wall over two thousand years ago, what more could be learned from the Chinese, immersed in the wisdom of the motherland?

∽

As 1995 came to a close, the Chen family traveled to Florida for a week-long family vacation. It was the week before Christmas and both Tei Fu and Oi-Lin were in particular need of rest.

The year had begun with all the intensity and difficulty surrounding the indictments on the tax and customs case. Then followed the spectacular Grand Convention in China. It had been the highlight of the year, but was an event that had required months of intensive efforts, both in preparation and follow-up. "It was a very difficult year," Chen concluded. "We began at a low point and then soared to new heights." That seemed to pretty well characterize the pattern of Sunrider's history.

The Chens looked forward to a week in the Florida sun with their children. It would give them a chance to relax and to reflect. It had been almost twenty-two years to the day since Tei Fu had arrived in Utah during a December snow storm. He much preferred the Florida sunshine.

∽

As the Chens relaxed in Florida, the snow was again falling in Utah. At the base of the majestic Wasatch Mountains, in the foothills overlooking the Provo/Orem valley, snow fell lightly on a fresh, unmarked grave in a secluded cemetery surrounded by tall pine trees.

Tei Fu does not have the ability to relax for long, and in Florida spent hours each day on the phone. One day he felt impressed to call his office in Taiwan. His call was directed to a cousin who worked in the Sunrider office there. The cousin told Chen that he was sorry about his father's death.

"What do you mean?" Chen shouted. "My father isn't dead. He's in Utah with my mother and sisters."

"So, they still haven't told you," his cousin replied.

Tei Fu quickly placed a call to his sister Jau-Fang, who also lived in Utah. "Father is OK," she said hopefully. She, too, was unaware.

The next call Chen placed was to his mother. "Yes," she said, "your father is dead." He had died two weeks before Christmas on December 11, 1995 of lung cancer. Chen desperately asked his mother why nobody had told him. "The dead are dead," his mother said flatly.

If his mother's words were cold and unfeeling, her tone was even more so. It was a tone of distance and irreconciliation.

In the following months, Tei Fu and Jau-Fang worked aggressively to learn the details of their father's passing. He had suffered with the cancer for weeks before his death. Chen's parents lived with Jau-Fei, and it was at her home where he had died. One of Chen's uncles, who spoke no English, had been flown from Taiwan to take care of him during his final weeks. There had been a small memorial service. Chen was told that Jau-Fei was not with her father when he died. Nor had she attended the funeral service on December 15.

The more Chen learned about the circumstances of his father's death, the more his sorrow turned to anger. His mind was filled with "why" questions. Why hadn't he been told of the cancer? Why had he not been notified of the death? Why hadn't he or Jau-Fang been allowed to attend the funeral? Why was there no obituary in the paper (a custom in China as much as in the West)? Why was the burial site at an unmarked grave, secreted away in a remote part of the cemetery? Tei Fu blamed the secrecy on his sister, Jau-Fei, and was suspicious of her motives.

Ever since Sunrider had sued E. Excel five years earlier for unfair competition, Jau-Fei had increasingly sought to position herself as a cancer researcher, and her company as a cancer research institute. In E. Excel corporate literature it states that "Jau-Fei performed more than ten years of cancer research" before founding E. Excel in 1987. (Since Jau-Fei was only twenty-six at the time E. Excel was founded, apparently she considered her school studies from age sixteen to be cancer research!)

In her lectures, Jau-Fei discussed the topic of "Nutritional Immunology," a science which she claims to have "created," and in which she postulates that with proper nutrition, rest, and exercise a person could live to be one hundred and twenty years old. "If you can do all three," she lectured, "I'll at least guarantee you one hundred and ten years old if not a hundred and twenty." Her father Yung-Yeuan Chen, was sixty-eight years old when he died. He lived at Jau-Fei's home.

When Oi-Lin was diagnosed with cancer in 1989, some E. Excel distributors had been unmerciful in ascribing her cancer to Sunrider products. Did Jau-Fei fear retribution? Was Jau-Fei fearful of losing face? "To have not informed me of my father's death, to not allow me to see him before he died, was very painful to me," Chen reflects. "For Jau-Fei to not fly home to be at his bedside or attend his funeral, is incomprehensible to me. If she could not arrange a flight, then why not charter a plane? Most upsetting to me though, is that they kept my father at my sister's home, allowed him to suffer and die there, rather than putting him in a hospital where he could have had proper care and medication. I know that my father's life was spent. But he did not deserve to die that way."

Jau-Fang committed to her brother that she would do whatever was necessary to locate their father's grave. Like her brother, she too wanted to pay final respect. Three months later, Tei Fu, Oi-Lin and their five children, along with Jau-Fang and her family, and accompanied by Marv and Geneva Peterson, walked through the lonely cemetery searching for their father's grave. They walked with wreaths of flowers and heavy hearts. They had a difficult time locating the grave site. It had no headstone—just a small metal marker.

Marv offered to dedicate the grave and to consecrate it as the resting place for the mortal body of Yung-Yeuan Chen. Tei Fu then knelt next to his father's grave to give a family prayer. As he began to express the words of his heart, his voice began to break and he started to cry. Cries turned into sobs as his chest heaved with the bitter pain and sorrow. He wept as a child—hard and uncontrollably.

He wept as only a son can at the grave of a father.

His wounds were deep and painful and he had been denied the chance to heal them before his father's death.

He wondered now if they could ever heal. He worried that they would not.

The families walked from the grave site in silence. There was a sense of finality, but not a sense of closure. Like many children who walk from cemeteries, Tei Fu wished that he had told his father that he loved him. He wished he could have forgiven his father, and asked for his forgiveness in return. Years later, when Dr. Chen and I visited one night at his home, I asked him if the wounds had ever healed. How does one make peace, I silently wondered, with the father who publicly denounced you, testified against you, and allowed himself to be used by those who sought to destroy you?

"No," he said to me, "the wounds have not healed."

"If you had been at his bedside before he died, what would you have said to him?" I asked.

He answered softly, "I would tell him I'm sorry."

CHAPTER TWENTY-TWO

Opportunity for a Lifetime

Attending the 1995 convention in China and witnessing the unbridled enthusiasm of the distributors generated a new level of hope and excitement within Tei Fu Chen. The message of health *and* wealth resonated in China. The Chinese people embraced the Sunrider products, philosophies, and particularly the money-making opportunity. Sometimes thousands of people would line up and pack themselves into Sunrider meetings. Security and crowd control became a major planning issue. Meetings were typically overflowing with standing-room only. Products were scooped up as fast as they became available.

Dr. Chen had actively encouraged his non-Chinese distributors to attend the Grand Convention in China. He wanted to show China's progressive development and culture to all the Western distributors and help them see that the Chinese are not professionally limited to restaurants and laundry shops. His hope was that the many seasoned Sunrider distributors could provide leadership to the inexperienced but enthusiastic Chinese. From feedback he received after the convention, it appeared that the Sunriders visiting China, rather than the Chinese, were the primary beneficiaries of the trip.

One U.S. distributor expressed a widely held sentiment in a letter to the Chens: "I appreciated the entertainment and spectacle of the convention, but particularly seeing the impact of Sunrider in emerging market economies such as China, Latvia, and Russia. Not only have you brought the best of Eastern culture to us, but you are now bringing the best of Western business to the East. I really heard your message about health *and* prosperity!"

The Grand Convention in China reinforced what Tei Fu already knew: Everywhere in the world, regardless of the country, the culture, or the economic status of the people, *everyone* has an interest in the opportunity to make money. For most, it is not so much an expectation of wealth as it is a yearning for the *freedom* and liberation that financial independence brings.

Through its products, Sunrider was enabling people to enjoy health and the opportunity for a quality of life they otherwise likely would not have. For most people, it was more than a new car or home. It was more than prosperity or a secure retirement fund. Sunrider was enabling thousands of people to have the independence of working for themselves, being their own boss, and being generously and fairly rewarded for the work they did.

If money has universal appeal, so does superior quality. On one occasion I asked Dr. Chen why he had chosen to buy a luxurious beach-front home in Hawaii since he spent, at most, only a few weeks a year there. Wouldn't it be better just to rent a property when he and his family were in Hawaii? He answered that the home was an *investment*.

Wasn't he concerned about the volatility of the real estate market? I asked. "Remember one thing before you ever invest in anything," he counseled me. "*Always* buy the best. The value of common things may rise or fall. But there is always a market for *the best*."

At Sunrider, convention themes are typically much more than a slogan for a meeting. In essence, they become the marketing strategy and the "branding position" for the company for a given year. The theme is the focus. "Sunrider, Simply the Best!" "Opportunity of a Lifetime . . . For a Lifetime." These messages of superior quality and lifetime opportunity were not only the themes for the 1996 and 1997 conventions, they were also messages at the core of Sunrider's mission statement.

American and worldwide acceptance of herbal nutritional products had by the mid-1990s skyrocketed. From pharmaceutical manufacturers to network-marketing companies to grocery stores, herbal foods, herbal beverages, and herbal supplements were being promoted everywhere. It had become nearly impossible to pick up a magazine or a newspaper, or to listen to the radio or watch TV, without hearing about some new herbal product or health discovery. Even Sunrider's health concepts like the Philosophy of Regeneration and the importance of whole food nutrition were receiving widespread media attention.

Those who had believed in the 1980s that Sunrider was "too extreme" to have broad-base appeal began to realize during the decade of the '90s that Sunrider was years ahead of the rest of the pack. On the issues of quality and exclusivity, Sunrider remains in a league of its own.

The mainstream interest in herbs and nutrition inspired the development of dozens of new products. More than just an herb-food company, Sunrider had progressed as a "total health company." Sunrider literature promoted products designed to "help people drink healthy, eat healthy,

look healthy, and live healthy." The concepts of regeneration, balance and harmony continued to be the philosophies upon which the Sunrider nutritional and personal care
products were based.

Meeting worldwide demand for the world's most
advanced and exclusive health products became a significant
Sunrider challenge. At times, production capacity simply
could not meet consumer demand. The Chens absolutely
refused to allow any of their products to be manufactured
outside of their own facilities, out of their own control.
Sunrider's superior quality assurances, as well as the company's reputation, was based in large part upon the superior
quality of the Sunrider products. Construction thus began
rapidly on new manufacturing facilities throughout Asia.

From a competitive standpoint, Sunrider held most of
the aces. In developing marketing strategies, marketing
experts sometimes say, "Be first or be best or be different."
Indisputably, Sunrider could claim all three. Tei Fu Chen
wanted to once again take Sunrider to the "next level." To
do so, he would have to do more than expand production
capacity. His challenge was to broaden the vision of Sunrider's fiercely loyal consumers, and help them see that the
world's greatest products . . . create the world's greatest
financial opportunities.

∽

On December 28, 1997, I was glad to be boarding an airplane for Hawaii. The weather on Oahu's north shore at Turtle
Bay was wet and windy, but still a welcome escape from the
frigid cold of a Utah winter.

Several hundred Sunrider leaders from many countries had once again gathered for three days of Group Director training, and to celebrate New Year's Eve on a cruise boat off Waikiki.

The tax and customs case was hardly an issue, and rarely mentioned. I felt relieved to attend a Sunrider meeting and not have to devote a majority of my time to providing distributors with updates on the status of the case.

The Turtle Bay training meetings were to be the only time in the upcoming year when Dr. Chen would be able to conduct any personal training.

The speech he delivered, and those of several other top leaders, were some of the most powerful and succinct distillations of the Sunrider story I had ever heard. Chen used no notes or visual aids—he just stood up and spoke from his heart. The usual jokes and audience interaction were put aside. He wanted only to share the lessons that he had learned through sixteen years of Sunrider experience.

Anyone who wanted a deeper understanding of Sunrider's past success, or to learn how to succeed as part of Sunrider's future, paid very close attention on New Year's Eve 1997.

The following are the core business beliefs of Tei Fu Chen—his wisdom, and his vision for Sunrider's future, spoken as only Tei Fu Chen could do. The message, delivered at Turtle Bay, is the essence of Sunrider's success.

Dr. Tei Fu Chen: What is Sunrider's greatest strength? Having the world's finest herbal products. What is Sunrider's greatest weakness? Having the world's greatest herbal products. Why do I say that? Because until we can see the potential opportunity that Sunrider provides beyond our products, we limit our ability to move forward into the next millennium.

How can Sunrider attract dynamic business builders? We have to talk about the money-making potential of Sunrider. There is a lot of competition in the world today. It's becoming increasingly hard to make money legitimately. It is much easier for some to deceive people. Should we lie like some of our competitors do? Let's just tell the truth. Our truth is far more compelling that their deceptions. People want to know more than just how good Sunrider is. People want to know why we're better than our competitors. We must do comparison. Tell them today how great Sunrider is and they'll believe you. Tomorrow, someone else will come along and they'll likely believe them. Prepare them today for what they will hear tomorrow.

Why network marketing? Because of the power of duplication. If you want to find success in multi-level marketing, it is not determined by how many people you sign up—but by how well you duplicate. Many people in network marketing do business the old-fashioned way. They buy and sell products. They don't invest! People are far more interested in learning about investment opportunities than they are about *sales* opportunities. People will turn off the business opportunity if they think they have to sell. If your prospect thinks that you're promoting a sales opportunity, then they'll say "Just tell me about the products." The prospect will force you to talk about the products first if they think that you want to talk about a sales opportunity.

When the economy goes bad, people think more and more about ways to make money, about opportunity, about solutions to their financial predicaments. Ten percent of the people are truly interested in products only. Ninety percent of the people are interested in products and the money-making opportunity.

Most people want quick and easy money. The "quick money people" will fail. They don't have a long-term thought. If the guy wants to jump in the lake, let him go. Don't let him pull you in with him.

The ability to succeed is not determined by one's educational degree. It's not even intelligence or experience. It comes down to common sense. Highly successful people are usually not the most educated people. Too much intelligence and a person gets contaminated by the system. Less-educated people use common sense. They think more simply. Students with "A" grades become doctors. Students with "B" grades become teachers. Students with "C" grades become rich.

What is the most common trait of all successful people? They're excited! Excitement doesn't come from pep rallies or motivational speakers. True excitement, the kind that really motivates people, comes from sponsoring—from sharing with others the good things that you have already found. Those who achieve the higher ranks in Sunrider sometimes become less inclined to sponsor. They want to spend their time teaching. This is a bad example. Once they quit sponsoring, how can they stay excited? How can they make others believe that sponsoring is the key when their example speaks louder than the words they teach?

Systems that really work and can be duplicated are built upon *simplicity* and *consistency*. Repeat your message to a lot of people and you can say the same thing over and over. Repeat your message to the same people over and over and it becomes much more complicated.

We have learned we must keep the product explanations very simple.

When comparing Sunrider to others, what are the most important points? It's not just what we have, it's also what the others don't have. Help people realize that they're taking a big chance, especially in the area of health, when they buy products from someone and they don't know who has manufactured them. Aren't we taught never to take candy from a stranger?

What is the Sunrider difference? We're a stable company who owns and controls our own manufacturing. We own our headquarters. Sunrider's owners have the expertise to manufacture the world's best products. We're committed to research and development and our concentrated products offer a greater value. Our marketing program is different. It's honest. It's fair. And it actually has rewarded millions of people.

Multi-level marketing can be good. It can be powerful. But only if you select the right company.

When you meet with a new prospect, you must be prepared to answer all of their questions. If he decides not to be part of Sunrider, it is his misfortune. If you can't respond— it is your misfortune.

It's more important to be a *product of the product* than it is to be an expert on the product.

Since food supports human life and since each human is a small universe, foods must conform to the natural laws of the universe. The basic rule of the universe is *harmony*. Harmony is a product of balance. Balance in the body requires eating the right combination of foods. Foods should be modeled after the universe, which balances the five elements to achieve harmony. The universe can live without us. We *can't* live without the universe. We must learn how to live with the universe. The Chinese approach to research is different from most of the rest of the world's. Chinese experiment on humans. The sample size—millions. The time frame of the test—over periods of thousands of years.

Why don't we simply grind up our herbs like others? Why does Sunrider transform herbs to juice? First, it becomes much easier to digest. Second, we are able to concentrate our products. Third, it's easier to preserve the natural character of the herbs. And whole foods always work better than isolated chemicals like vitamin pills.

People enjoy hearing other people's personal stories. Share your own. Listen to theirs. Make your presentations interactive. Let people experience our products. Be open to questions. Be personal. Do demonstrations. Find common ground. Be willing to share your goals, your desires, the things you hope for in life.

How important is it for a company to have owners who have expertise? It's this simple. We have products that *work*. We have products that are *safe*. We have products that have *integrity*. As an example goldenseal root has many positive benefits. Some goldenseal root, however, can be very harmful to women. It can shrink the uterus. A company needs to use the right goldenseal root. Who do you trust to make that choice? Who do you trust with your health? Who do you trust with the health of your family?

Invite your friends over for some Chinese food and share with them the Sunrider products.

In the corporate world, whoever has a great idea protects it. They want the credit for themselves. In the competitive market place, ideas become property and are copyrighted, patented and marketed on tapes and videos and books. In the Sunrider world, great ideas are shared—liberally, unselfishly, gladly.

For nearly twenty years, Sunrider has consistently grown and prospered. We have survived every form of challenge and overcome every obstacle that would break the backs of all but the strongest. Why do we survive? Because of the quality of our products! Our products work! The typical person doesn't care about our legal problems. They care only whether our products work and whether they're going to be available.

We've learned how to succeed as a product-driven company. To move forward into the next millennium, we must become an "opportunity-driven company." Today, Sunrider already offers the greatest money-making opportunity in the world. And most people don't even know it. How can I say that? How can I say that we have the world's greatest opportunity? Because we have the world's greatest products. *The quality of any opportunity is determined by the quality of the product that it stands upon.*

For most of the previous sixteen years, Tei Fu Chen had traveled the world sharing his strategies, his products, and the Sunrider opportunity. In all, he had spoken in over two hundred cities in thirty countries on all seven continents of the world. Over two million people had signed on as Sunrider distributors.

In recognition of their international distributors, the Sunrider convention in 1998 had been themed "Around the World with Sunrider." Hundreds of people were planning to attend from China as well as from other countries with emerging economies such as Hungary, Eastern Europe, Latvia, and the Philippines, where the Sunrider potential had yet to be tapped. Hundreds of Chinese distributors were looking forward to their first trip to America. In just four years Sunrider had grown to be the leading multi-level marketing company in China.

However, the hopes of the Chinese distributors were dampened, and Sunrider was put on temporary hold, when in April 1998 the Chinese government banned all multi-level marketing in the country.

The ban was not directed at Sunrider, or other credible multi-level marketing companies that were following ethical business practices in China. But literally hundreds of "get rich quick" schemes had proliferated in China under the broad banner of "network marketing." The Chinese government decided to ban all MLM companies until it could determine a plan of action that would allow the legitimate long-term companies to re-establish operations. Although a setback to Sunrider and its distributors in China, the Chens believed that over the long haul, the government ban would be to the benefit of the company. Sunrider had invested millions of dollars in China with a commitment to be there for generations to come. That was the Sunrider way.

One other prominent Sunrider would not be able to attend the 1998 Grand Convention. His name was Tei Fu Chen. For the first time in Sunrider's sixteen-year history, Dr. Chen would miss the Grand Convention.

On March 10, 1998, Dr. Chen was scheduled to begin a two-year term of confinement at the Federal Detention Camp in Boron, California.

CHAPTER TWENTY-THREE

Failed Justice

The headline on the news release dated March 1, 1995 from the United States Attorney, Central District of California, read: "Torrance Health Food Company and Its Owners Indicted in Massive Tax and Customs Fraud Scheme."

A variation of that headline was to run in newspapers throughout the United States. The news release was also posted on the Internet, for all the world to see. Some of the language in the press release sounded more like a politician's campaign speech than a legal announcement from the Justice Department:

"Those who manipulate and abuse our system of voluntary reporting, through sophisticated means of international chicanery, can expect to be investigated, caught and prosecuted. We will not tolerate tax cheats." The press release outlined the details of the twenty-count indictment, and concluded that if found guilty, Tei Fu Chen faced a possible prison sentence of eighty-seven years.

At issue was the business relationship between Sunrider and Paget, the company that was created in the early years of Sunrider by Oi-Lin's father, to locate suppliers of raw herbs and to oversee quality control and the initial processing of the herbs before they were shipped to Sunrider.

Besides the fact that Papa Tsui had initially provided some of the start-up capital for Sunrider, Paget had played a legitimate and critical role in Sunrider's early success. When Sunrider sales boomed in the mid-1980s, no one could argue that Paget and Oi-Lin's family were entitled to a share of Sunrider's financial success.

The government would argue that the money paid to Paget was excessive for the services provided. The debate was reduced to a simple question: How does one determine the value of the contributions of Oi-Lin's father (and subsequently her brother, Man Tat) to Sunrider's success? If the case went to trial, it was expected that tax and accounting experts would debate the fair market value of the Tsui family's efforts, whether the accountants had been sufficiently advised of relevant facts, and whether the professional advice given to Sunrider by lawyers and accountants was reasonable.

These extraordinarily complicated tax issues, referred to as "transfer pricing," are issues which most major companies doing international business must address. In Sunrider's first two years, accounting functions were handled largely in-house by Jau-Hwa Chen. In 1985, the issues had become so complex, Sunrider hired a "Big Six" accounting firm, Ernst & Whinney (now Ernst & Young). The government charged that because Sunrider was calculating and paying Paget's invoices at "higher than fair market value" dollar amounts, Ernst & Whinney were misled into entering inflated "cost of goods sold" figures as business expenses on tax returns, thereby understating the Chens' and Sunrider's taxable income.

The case was to be even more complex. When Jau-Hwa left Sunrider and took with her the Sunrider documents, Sunrider filed an unfair competition lawsuit against E. Excel. It was Sunrider's contention, as stated by legal counsel Vincent Marella, that Jau-Hwa and Jau-Fei responded in part to Sunrider's lawsuit by contacting the

IRS and the U.S. Attorney's office, "lobbying them to bring pressure on Sunrider and Tei Fu Chen by opening an investigation. The Chen sisters succeeded. In late 1990, the IRS opened a civil tax audit of Sunrider, and IRS criminal investigators began analyzing records which Jau-Hwa had taken from Sunrider. The audit eventually led to the IRS filing notices of deficiency for the years 1984 through 1991.

"The Customs Service got involved to determine whether Sunrider paid too much money to Customs in duties [to avoid higher tax liabilities] and later to determine if Tei Fu Chen had understated the value of certain antiques he brought into the company (*even though the antiques were not dutiable*)."

Thus was the background that led to the filing of the criminal indictments against Sunrider, and Tei Fu and Oi-Lin Chen, on March 1, 1995.

Sunrider released a prepared statement of its own on the day the indictments were filed. In contrast to the Assistant U.S. Attorney's inflammatory rhetoric, the language of Richard Richards, Sunrider's general counsel, was tempered and matter-of-fact.

> The basis of this case is, simply stated, a legitimate tax dispute complicated by the fact that Sunrider does business in over twenty countries. During the past four years of investigation the company has fully cooperated with the government. For over two years now, these issues have been actively litigated and substantial progress has been made. Of the approximately one hundred items of dispute, eighty-two

have already been resolved. The remaining issues are pending in the U.S. Tax Court which is realistically where this case belongs.

Throughout its history, Sunrider has created thousands of jobs, has paid tens of millions of dollars in taxes, and has conducted its business affairs with commitment and integrity. Given the complexities of managing a rapidly growing international business, Sunrider has consistently retained and relied upon leading tax and customs attorneys and Big Six accounting firms.

Despite today's developments, Mr. and Mrs. Chen have asked that I express their profound belief in the U.S. Justice system. The Chens are very proud to be naturalized U.S. citizens and are justifiably proud of the success of their company.

Mortimer Caplin, a former commissioner of the Internal Revenue Service, would later review and voice full agreement with Richard Richards' assessment of the case. Caplin wrote: "The government's case against Mr. Chen was based primarily on the application of unusually complicated rules and regulations in the tax code . . . indeed in my years in government service and private practice, I have never seen the government criminally prosecute a transfer pricing case. Such cases are routinely pursued as civil tax matters."

Dick Richards added, "People understand that almost every large successful company, especially those doing international business, eventually has to do battle with the IRS. It's just a shame that in this case an ambitious young Assistant U.S. Attorney chose to pursue it criminally rather than through the civil courts, which is where it belonged."

∾

I left Los Angeles to return to Salt Lake City on the last flight of the night on March 1, 1995. I sat in the airplane's dimly lit cabin immersed in thought, feeling a great sense of despair. The injustice of the indictments against the Chens was simply incomprehensible. It offended me to the very core. Would this be the end of the Chens' pursuit of the American Dream? How would the likely damage to Sunrider's image affect the lives and livelihoods of Sunrider's thousands of distributors and employees? What happened that day was more far-reaching than a tax or customs case. It was an assault upon the lives of many, many people, especially of course, Tei Fu and Oi-Lin Chen.

∾

The Chens' continued belief and confidence in the U.S. Justice system was magnanimous, given the heavy-handedness of many government officials during the previous three years, and which continued through the Chens' arraignment. The prosecutor, Assistant U.S. Attorney George Newhouse, asked the judge to set bond for the Chens at a colossal $20 million each and requested that they be required to forfeit their passports and only be allowed to travel with Newhouse's permission. He called the Chens "risks for flight." The judge didn't buy the prosecutor's argument, and set bail at a fraction of what he had asked. Recognizing the dynamics of the Chens' business, he also allowed them to continue to travel internationally as necessary.

On occasion, I had been asked by people familiar with the case if I believed it possible that Dr. Chen might simply leave the United States and not return. After all, he could lead a very comfortable life in many other countries and considering all of the tribulation to which he had been subjected in the United States, simply leaving could be easily justified.

There was not even a flicker of doubt in my mind. I knew that there was no circumstance whatsoever that could motivate him to flee. Nevertheless one day I brought up the subject with Mrs. Chen.

"Whoever would ask such a question does not know my husband's character," she answered sharply. "He loves America. Our children are American. He would never do such a thing to our American distributors. My husband is not a quitter!"

What Mrs. Chen said was true. I felt embarrassed that I had even raised the question, and apologized.

In my experience with Tei Fu Chen, I have seen his imperfections and occasionally have believed that he has made poor choices. But never once in the twelve years that I have known Chen have I ever observed an action on his part that I felt was improper or dishonest. In the countless hours I have spent with him, I cannot recall a single instance when he said or did something that caused me to respect him less. He is a man of solid character and those who know him well have always been willing to stand by him.

                                    ∽

Few people understand the grand jury system and realize that indictments are issued after the jury has only heard one side of the story—the prosecutor's case. A grand jury consists of ordinary people called to jury service, who are required to convene periodically and listen to hours of tedious testimony presented by whatever witnesses *the prosecutor* chooses to summon. Defense lawyers are not allowed to call witnesses or submit evidence. Defense lawyers are not allowed to cross-examine any witnesses. Defense lawyers are not even allowed in the hearing room. Most legal scholars would agree with Dick Richards' assessment of the grand jury system. "If the prosecutor wants it to, a grand jury will indict a ham sandwich."

Nevertheless, grand jury indictments make great news headlines and every prosecutor is well aware of that reality. Indicting someone is, in many respects, far more punitive than actually convicting them. Especially if the indictments generate big news. Once a person is charged with a crime, they are in reality tried in the news media. There is no due process. An individual's name and reputation can be forever tainted.

Most people who read news stories assume that there must be some basis of fact or the person would have never been charged. In a tragic distortion of the "American way," we assume a person is guilty unless they are exonerated, especially if the person is wealthy, an Asian immigrant, and the case deals with complicated tax issues. To make matters worse, when the chief accuser is a member of your own family, your presumed guilt is likely a foregone conclusion.

Big cases like Sunrider's have the potential to launch

careers. Especially for young aggressive prosecutors. Although
Roger Olsen, Mrs. Chen's attorney on the case, offered assur-
ance that the Justice Department does not allow its prosecutors to try their cases in the news media, *someone* was certainly
interested that the indictments of the Chens and Sunrider
receive as much exposure as possible. Within a matter of days
of the indictments, copies of the U.S. Attorney's press release
had been anonymously mailed to dozens of news organizations in several countries around the world.

∾

It came as no surprise to me when in August 1996 we
received a call from a *Wall Street Journal* reporter named
John Emshwiller. He had a long list of questions dealing
with familiar themes, including Chen's relationship with his
father, the Chinese manuscripts, whether Chen had a doctorate degree, and most of the other issues that had been
raised in the course of the Debi Boling litigation. In fact, he
said he had received a complete transcript of the Boling case
even though at that time the documents had been sealed by
the court. He asked for the opportunity to meet with the
Chens.

Although Dr. Chen's attorneys advised against it, Chen
said that he would be willing to meet with Emshwiller on
one condition—that the reporter first tour the City of
Industry manufacturing facility. He agreed, and like most
people came away from the tour with an entirely different
perspective of Sunrider.

He met with Dr. and Mrs. Chen on October 15 and
then spent the next ten weeks preparing his article which

ran as a front-page feature story in *The Wall Street Journal* on January 7, 1997. The copy surrounded an artist's sketch of Tei Fu and Oi-Lin Chen. The article had two headlines, one of which was "Calm Eludes Sunrider's Herbal Empire." The story read:

> In the office of Tei Fu Chen stands a cabinet with dozens of small drawers filled with roots, leaves, powders— a little storehouse of herbs. It hardly looks like a launching pad for a global business empire.
>
> But the forty-eight-year-old Taiwan native has mixed, mashed and cooked his herbs into some one hundred products—teas, cosmetics, food supplements—sold around the world. He and his wife, Oi-Lin, sell about $700 million worth of them a year through their wholly owned Sunrider Corporation, thanks to the efforts of more than a million independent distributors scattered through twenty-five countries. . . . Mr. Chen's formula is simple. He says: Give people a chance to achieve "health and wealth" through Sunrider.
>
> Actually though, Mr. Chen's world is hardly simple. His herbs to riches saga is spiced with enough controversy and discord to fill a potboiler, and much of it has been provided by his own family. His father once took the witness stand against him during a suit by an unhappy customer. One of his sisters heads a rival company that has traded lawsuits with Sunrider. Another sister is trying to put Mr. Chen in prison.

The story continued with a thorough review of the tax and customs case. On the whole, the article was both balanced and accurate. It *was* the story of Sunrider.

∾

From the time of the indictments, building the case against the Chens was to be spread out over two and a half years. The process became, and was likely designed to be, far more brutal than what the eventual outcome of the case would be.

The raids at the Chens' home and at their office headquarters had greatly impacted both their employees and their family. Prosecutor Newhouse continued to use the grand jury to contact employees, former employees, family members, distributors, former distributors, virtually anyone who could offer anything to help build his case. The biases of Newhouse were obvious to almost anyone who dealt with him. As Dick Richards put it, "Pure and simple, the prosecutor believes that the Chens are evil. He has said it on more than one occasion. His investigation has not been the pursuit of truth, it has been the pursuit of prosecution and persecution."

Eventually his heavy-handed and abusive tactics were more than the Sunrider legal team could tolerate.

Roger Olsen, who had been retained to represent Oi-Lin, was a tall, ruddy, serious lawyer. A former Deputy Attorney General in the Justice Department in Washington, D.C., Olsen was not only a very experienced attorney, he had a deep understanding of the inner workings of the Justice Department. Being a no-nonsense prosecutor, he was well aware of the ethical standards that federal judges expect from those who have been empowered with the public trust. One prominent federal judge characterized the prosecutor's responsibility this way: "Prosecutors are subject to constraints and responsibilities that don't apply to other lawyers . . . the prosecutor's job isn't just to win, but to win fairly, staying well within the rules."

In late 1996, Olsen filed a thirty-three page motion, outlining the pattern of government misconduct in the tax and customs case. Olsen outlined nine specific instances of alleged abuse of power by the government.

In his brief to the United States District Court, Olsen said:

> The prosecutors exploited racial animus to whip up anti-Asian feeling among Grand Jurors, building upon a bias that was first displayed by Customs agents during their search of the Sunrider Corporation. The prosecutors repeatedly made false statements to the court and to defense counsel. The government blatantly and repeatedly invaded Sunrider's attorney/client privilege . . . Customs agents deliberately attempted to intimidate the Chens' children and employees in executing search warrants of the Chens' home and business, and threatened to destroy their property under the pretext of searching for contraband . . . the government systematically invaded the privacy of grand jury witnesses by obtaining their confidential tax returns, in violation of the law, and scrutinizing the returns for information that might be used as leverage against the witnesses.

Olsen documented three instances where both the Assistant United States Attorney and the chief Customs agent had engaged in apparent racial bias against the Chens because of their Asian heritage. In one instance, an outside accountant who had worked for Sunrider was asked by the Assistant U.S. Attorney why there was not a formal written contract between Tei Fu Chen and his father-in-law. The accountant testified in front of the grand jury that verbal agreements, along with a handshake, are "very typical in dealings between Asian parties." The government prosecutor responded so all could hear, "So is fraud." His intemperate remarks suggested a bias that fraud is typical in dealings between Asians. Olsen continued, "It is truly shocking that a federal prosecutor, sworn to uphold the principle of equal justice before the law, would make such a remark."

The lead Customs agent, in executing a search warrant on Sunrider's headquarters in 1993, also displayed obvious prejudice against Asians. In one employee's deposition it was cited that during the search, the agent referred to Chen as "the big koi fish." The comment was indicative of the anti-Chinese bias that was shown in many instances during the course of the Sunrider investigation.

Olsen also pointed out that Jau-Hwa, Dr. Chen's sister, would likely be called as the chief government witness in the case. For months, the U.S. Attorney's office had represented to both the defendants and the court that "No promises of any kind, including no promises or assurances of any form for immunity, have ever been made to Jau-Hwa by the government, nor to the government's knowledge has Jau-Hwa asked for formal or informal immunity." The prosecutor made a similar claim in another federal court in July 1995. "Jau-Hwa has never asked for any reward, payment or other monetary remuneration in return for her information."

Months later, the government reluctantly produced a letter dated July 3, 1990 from Jau-Hwa's attorney to the government in which Jau-Hwa had not only *requested immunity* but had also advised the government that she would seek an *informer's reward* from the IRS.

During the time that Jau-Hwa had worked for Sunrider, from 1983 through 1990, she had served as the company's controller. When she left Sunrider to join E. Excel, she took with her many internal and confidential documents that she had taken from Sunrider to use in her sister's new company and to use against her brother. It was unclear whether she was afraid of her own vulnerability to an IRS investigation, or whether she simply wanted to create a nightmare for her brother with the IRS. Either way, she apparently got what she wanted. As of 1990, documents revealed that the federal government was in the process of granting Jau-Hwa immunity in exchange for her testimony against her brother.

As a former government prosecutor and a man of impeccable integrity, Roger Olsen was highly reluctant to accuse government representatives of having engaged in misconduct. However, after months of review and years of documentation, he could not help but reach the conclusion which he articulated in his motion:

> *The government's conduct tainted the entire grand jury process and corrupted the fair and even-handed administration of criminal justice.*
>
> This motion was not brought lightly. While defense counsel on this case have tremendous respect for the Justice Department, the facts of this case, unfortunately, make the filing of this motion necessary. The due process clause of the Constitution and the integrity of the judicial system require

this court to act in the face of outrageous and pervasive government misconduct.

The entire investigation and prosecution of this case has been pervaded and corrupted by the government's manifestly improper conduct. These abusive tactics are outrageous, shocking and fundamentally unfair.

These were very serious allegations. For Roger Olsen to file such a motion and to speak in such strong language showed how deeply he believed that the Chens, their family, and Sunrider had been subjected to extreme prosecutorial abuse.

The civil tax case was settled long before the criminal case would ever be concluded. In essence, the IRS and Sunrider both compromised and met each other half way. Many of the tax deductions that Sunrider had claimed were allowed—others were not. With the civil tax case settled, Sunrider attorneys could now focus entirely on settling the criminal case.

In a surprising and highly unusual move, senior officials at the Justice Department in Washington, D.C., contacted Sunrider's attorneys in February 1997 with a proposal. Rather than proceed to trial with the criminal case, why not allow a special "settlement court judge" to arbitrate the case. It was proposed that the judge would give both sides the opportunity to present their cases and then would meet with them to negotiate a settlement.

The Chens had a tough decision to make, one of the most difficult they would ever have to face. If they chose to go to trial, they would finally have their day in court. Despite the fact that the case was several years old, Sunrider had never had a chance to tell its side of the story. Sunrider's attorneys argued that it would be best to settle the case. At a trial, complicated evidence would be presented to a jury of common people who would have to wade through weeks and perhaps even months of witnesses and then make a decision on each of the twenty counts. Even if the Chens were found guilty on just one of the twenty counts, mandatory sentencing guidelines could require three to four years in prison for both Tei Fu and Oi-Lin.

Chen's sister Jau-Hwa would likely be the government's star witness. The attorneys worried that just as in the Boling case, if a family member is the accuser, jurors were likely to believe that there must be at least some element of truth to the charges. The Chens were reminded too of the O.J. Simpson trial. Often it is not the evidence that determines the outcome. To Tei Fu, the decision all came down to a single issue. If Oi-Lin could be spared the indignity of a trial and would not have to face the prospect of being incarcerated, Chen said he would be willing to settle the case. After weeks of negotiations, Judge Matt Byrne put an offer on the table and strongly encouraged both sides to accept the terms. It was to be his final offer.

Tei Fu and Oi-Lin would each plead guilty to a single count of tax evasion. Tei Fu additionally would plead guilty to one customs count. Sunrider would be fined and Tei Fu would be required to serve a twenty-four-month sentence at a federal detention camp. The deal was done.

I sat in on the meeting with Dr. and Mrs. Chen and their team of attorneys at which the terms of the settlement were discussed. Once Dr. Chen had agreed to the terms, everyone stood up and was prepared to leave. Dr. Chen called the group back into his office and asked everyone to sit down. "I have just one more question," Dr. Chen said. "Can any of you here tell me what I did wrong?" Initially no one said anything. Then one of the attorneys spoke up. His answer was a sad reflection on the American system of government. "The issue isn't whether you've done something wrong, Dr. Chen," the attorney said. "The only thing that matters is what a jury believes."

"I understand that," Dr. Chen said. "That's why I have chosen to settle this case. But I want to ask you one more time. Can anyone in this room please tell me what it is that I have done wrong?"

Again, the room was silent. No one could answer.

I too had a question. How were we going to explain to the world why the Chens had chosen to enter a guilty plea, even though they genuinely believed that they were innocent? Dr. Chen reminded me of the TruSweet case nearly fifteen years earlier. "We need to just stand up in front of the people and tell them the truth."

CHAPTER TWENTY-FOUR

The
Sunrider
Heart

By the time the tax and customs case had finally been settled, five long years had passed since the first raids at Sunrider's headquarters and at the Chens' home. It had been over seven years since Jau-Hwa had left Sunrider and first contacted the IRS.

The damage done by those who wield the awesome powers of government couldn't be measured alone by the impact upon the lives of the Chens, their children, or their Sunrider family, or by the millions of dollars Sunrider was forced to spend in legal fees. There was more. In the words of Raymond Donovan, a former cabinet member under President Ronald Reagan, who had been indicted and years later exonerated: "To which government office do you go to get your reputation back?"

By the spring of 1997, Dr. Chen had simply decided enough was enough. It was time to settle. Chen was willing to bear the brunt of the pain, even at the personal cost of incarceration. He believed closing the case was in the best long-term interests of everyone involved with Sunrider. Dr. Chen considered the settlement a *business* decision.

I knew there was much more to it, and how Chen had anguished over the pain of his wife, children, and Sunrider family. I watched him look at Oi-Lin during the meetings with attorneys as settlement options were discussed. It was the same look that I had seen him give Oi-Lin when the two had danced in Hong Kong five years earlier on their twentieth wedding anniversary—a look of deep love, uncompromised by years of stress and sorrow.

In a series of meetings just before the 1997 Grand

Convention, the Chens, Dick Richards, and I discussed the settlement of the case with distributor leaders, country managers, and Sunrider employees. Dick and I explained the convoluted details of the case. Both Dr. and Mrs. Chen stood and expressed themselves with calm, dignity, and great compassion. We all spoke at length and with much emotion.

Mrs. Chen told me of a distributor who had voiced frustration about the tax case. A few of the distributor's downline group had decided to drop out of Sunrider, citing the negative publicity surrounding the case. "They're bleeding on the outside," Mrs. Chen said to me. "I'm bleeding on the inside."

The overwhelming majority of distributors, including virtually every one of the leaders, stood solidly behind the Chens' decision. Many stood up in meetings to express their unqualified support and love for the Chens. Many of them had been with Sunrider since the very beginning, and each had contributed greatly to Sunrider's success. Each understood the meanings of "commitment" and "sacrifice."

In one meeting, a Chinese distributor called the burden that Dr. Chen would continue to bear "heavy stones upon Chen's shoulders." "If I could," he said, "I would carry the boulders. Then, when we came to the next stream of water obstructing our path, I would lay them down and use them as stepping stones."

I had tremendous respect for every one of these people. Without a doubt, they were the very heart of Sunrider.

∾

After the 1997 convention, Mrs. Chen and I were talking about the tremendous outpouring of caring and support that had been extended to the Chens by the Sunrider distributors. "In what other company where a CEO has faced these kinds of challenges," she asked me, "do you find a group of people with such loyalty and commitment?"

"It says a lot about your husband," I responded.

"It also says a lot about our *distributors!*" she quickly added.

Sunrider distributors are in fact a unique group of people. When I first became associated with Sunrider in 1989, I assumed that the distributors are people who are into health foods, money, and network marketing. But I have learned over the years that, for the most part, money is *not* the primary motivator with a typical Sunrider distributor. These are people who live life with passion and purpose. They are men and women who have strived to achieve new heights in their own lives, and who have been driven and rewarded by helping others do the same. The Sunrider distributor wants to walk on the Great Wall of China—but will not be fulfilled unless ten others they have helped are walking beside them.

In the world of Sunrider, it is called "The Sunrider Heart." It's an approach to life and an attitude that has been both instilled and exemplified by Tei Fu and Oi-Lin Chen.

I remember the 1996 Grand Convention, when Dr. Chen explained to distributors the symbols of a Sunrider brand he had recently created. He had taken the letters "S" and "R" and forged them together in an artistic design. Dr. Chen explained:

> Please take a very close look at the new Sunrider brand, specifically at the upper half. You will see the image of a heart. I designed the brand that way for a reason. The brand stands for quality and opportunity. But most importantly, Sunrider is a business of the heart. People in Sunrider care about other people. The heart stands for integrity and loyalty. We promote opportunity and quality, but our message is effective only if it comes from the heart. Wear the pin with the Sunrider brand wherever you go. And always wear the pin on your left lapel, which is where it belongs—over your heart.

Dick Richards and I were given SR pins by the Chens. The pins are beautiful and distinctive, each in solid gold inset with three diamonds. In my life, I have on occasion received a pin as a form of recognition. There is only one pin I wear, however, and always on my left lapel.

❧

At the time of the indictments in 1995, the Assistant U.S. Attorney had warned dramatically that Dr. Chen could, if found guilty, be sentenced "up to eighty-seven years in prison." Oi-Lin could face "up to thirty-seven years."

In fact, Dr. Chen would spend a total of eleven months at the Detention Camp in Boron, California beginning in March 1998. Oi-Lin was required to fulfill a term of six months of home confinement. She was able to go to work every day and return home at night, and was required to receive permission before traveling.

"It's OK," she told distributors, "I've been doing home confinement ever since I got married twenty-five years ago!"

On September 4, 1997, the Chens were formally sentenced before a judge in downtown Los Angeles. I waited to field calls from the news media. None came. The closure of the case received but a small mention in only a few newspapers. It seemed that the case was much like the month of March—it came in as a lion and went out as a lamb. But there remained those who lurked in the shadows and continued trying to defame Sunrider through negative publicity. Within a few months of Dr. Chen's incarceration at Boron, many Asian news organizations in Southern California, as well as in China and Taiwan, received a heavy anonymous envelope in the mail (packets were also later anonymously distributed in Israel, Hungary, and in other thriving Sunrider markets). Over eighty-pages thick, the packet contained copies of the indictments against the Chens and court records of their guilty pleas, along with copies of news clippings covering the tax and customs case. Every page had been translated carefully to Chinese. On the cover of the packet was a copy of the photograph of Dr. Chen taken at the time he entered the Boron facility—an unflattering picture commonly referred to as a mug shot.

❧

The 1998 convention week was, in most respects, like many others. By day, there were training seminars, a product fair, and a ribbon cutting at Sunrider's impressive new Chinese-style botanical garden. By night, there were theme parties, festive dinners, and "family reunions" that senior distributors organized for their downline groups.

It was a convention unlike any other with Dr. Chen not there. He was missed. The most frequently asked question: "How is Dr. Chen doing?"

Mrs. Chen did a masterful job of managing and conducting the week. Many distributors saw a side of her that they had previously only glimpsed. She was warm, funny, and projected the confidence of an executive who bore the full mantle of leadership.

As usual, exciting new products were introduced. New country openings were announced—perhaps as many as fifteen within the next two or three years—and new construction was unveiled. Sunrider would add 50,000 square feet to its corporate headquarters, including the largest exhibit of Chinese art and artifacts in the Western hemisphere.

The president of Sunrider International also shared the Chens' vision of Sunrider's future. On the eve of a new millennium, and in a world of new technology, Dr. Oi-Lin Chen saw limitless potential. In the industries of herbal nutritionals and network marketing, Sunrider had always positioned itself as the technology leader. Once again, however, it was a time for change—to rise to the next level. She implored Sunrider distributors to broaden their vision, to look forward and see Sunrider as "a new leader . . . for a new millennium."

No one could dispute that throughout its seventeen-year history, Sunrider had emerged as a leader in the health and beauty industries. The company and its independent distributors had had a profound impact on the way millions of people view and manage their health. Equally important, Sunrider had enabled prosperity and financial freedom for tens of thousands of people in every corner of the world.

In ways that were impossible for Dr. and Mrs. Chen to comprehend in 1982, they had accomplished their goal of bringing together the best of East and West, of modern and traditional. Unlike some companies, Sunrider has never deviated from its mission of "health and prosperity." The American Dream has been fulfilled by a couple who built a company that met common needs in uncommon ways . . . and provided the opportunity for millions of others to achieve their goals and fulfill their dreams in the process.

On the cusp of the next thousand years, Oi-Lin concluded by sharing the Chens' hope "that Sunrider will be the journey of my children, and yours . . . that people everywhere, through Sunrider, can be elevated to new heights . . . to take people places that they've never been before."

"I watched one distributor from Asia on the stage," she added. "He was uneducated and, before Sunrider, had sold beef noodles on the street. Now he was wearing a suit. He was speaking to two thousand people. He was a new person. It made me feel that our sacrifices have purpose. It's like watching your children grow."

∽

On a Saturday in August, the 1998 convention came to a grand conclusion. The finale featured a video in which Tei Fu Chen paid tribute to his wife, his children, and his distributors. Mrs. Chen was joined on stage by her children, and the leaders of the "Sunrider family." A song was sung that had been written for the occasion, entitled "The Sunrider Heart." Every person in the massive arena stood and joined in singing "one mission . . . one purpose . . . one heart!"

The one person who could not join in the drama was Tei Fu Chen. He was, however, in the hearts and minds of everyone. Throughout the week, Dr. Chen had kept in touch over the telephone to share in each day's events.

With the convention just over, he called and we spoke again. I asked if it had been hard on him to miss the traditional event—to have only been remotely connected from afar.

"Oh, no," he said quickly.

"I'm excited!"

Epilogue

$\mathcal{J}$n June 1998, Mrs. Chen and I met in Provo, Utah, where she had traveled to pick up Sunny from college at BYU, and to arrange housing for the Chen children for the fall semester. The time had come to choose a theme for the convention scheduled fourteen months later in Pasadena, California. Mrs. Chen knew the convention message she wanted to convey, but wasn't exactly sure how to say it.

"It needs to be a message of life's struggles, of facing challenges, and overcoming adversity," she explained.

"What about words like 'trial' and 'triumph'?" I offered.

"No," she shook her head. She wanted to include the imagery of the sun. "Face the sun," she said, "and you find light and warmth. The shadow is put behind you."

"How about, 'Walk to the sun'?" I asked.

"No," she said. "Walking is too easy. No one's life is easy."

Oi-Lin had been reading a book entitled *The Miracle of Forgiveness* by Spencer W. Kimball, the Mormon prophet whom she had met nineteen years earlier, and whose advice on parenting she had never forgotten. He wrote of life being a journey, "[We] travel sometimes dangerously, sometimes safely, sometimes sadly, sometimes happily. Always the road is marked by divine purpose."

"Since life is a journey," Mrs. Chen concluded, "why not 'Journey to the Sun'?" A convention theme—and the title of this book—were born.

◌

When Dr. Chen began his stay at Boron, I resolved to visit him at least once a month. Most often, I would make the trip on a Sunday and join him, along with one other individual, at an LDS worship service the three of us held. We sat around a table in a small room, sang hymns accompanied by a cassette tape player, and read from a Mormon lesson manual. Dr. Chen talked of the great impact that his incarceration had on his most heartfelt beliefs:

> When I first came here, I wondered what had happened to me—why God would allow these things to happen. I did not believe I had done anything wrong. Slowly, I began to see His purpose.

> I had always believed I was a strong man with a strong will and a good mind. I began to see my many weaknesses. Through all the years I had worked so hard, I had been too busy. I never had one day to sit down and try to get closer to God—to sit down with Him.

> But I had always seen His hand in my life. When I had been in the military, I could hear His voice in my ears. When I needed to pass the exam to get into college, He helped me to find the answers. He led me to Paraguay and helped me walk through immigration into Brazil. He opened the door so that I could come to the United States. When I arrived in Salt Lake City and was lost, a stranger was prompted to come to me and offer help. He blessed me with a good wife and wonderful children. But I was always too busy to kneel down and pray and say thanks for what God has given to me.

I believe that's why I am here. Now I thank God for all of this. I find peace in reading His words. God has given me and my wife many challenges, but always He has shown us the path and walked beside us.

I find peace in knowing that He has never left me. He still loves me. I feel warmness in my heart and thank Him every day, in every step that I take.

∾

The days of microwaved chicken wings and drives across the Mojave Desert are over. During my regular visits with the Chens we once again meet and eat in their private dining room at Sunrider's headquarters. Their personal chef prepares colorful plates of fish and chicken, fresh fruits and vegetables. Of course there is always sticky rice, Fortune Delight—a popular Sunrider beverage—and Dr. Chen's Secret Sauce on the table. While we eat, we talk. Usually we discuss details of the next convention, themes and songs, videos, and CD-ROMs, trips to one continent or another, and media interviews. Dr. Chen offers samples of his latest product innovation. Mrs. Chen voices frustration over construction delays on the huge expansion of their corporate headquarters. The tax and customs case and Dr. Chen's time at Boron are rarely mentioned anymore. It's in the shadow.

One day, when the Chens were in a reflective mood, I asked if they had to do it all over again, would they follow the same path?

"Of course," Dr. Chen said. "From every experience there is a lesson to learn. But if we fail to learn, then usually we have to repeat the same experience. Obstacles will always be in our path. We grow strong when we climb. We grow wise when we fail."

Mrs. Chen added her view, saying something that I will never forget:

"We can't always choose the path we take. We can only choose whether we are going to be happy . . . or whether we will be sad."

ᕽ

Delta flight 324 flies from Los Angeles to Salt Lake City. It is my favorite trip because it's the trip *home.* If the evening sun is not obscured by clouds, and if I look closely, from the airplane's window I can spot the hillside, the water tower, and the scattered buildings of a bleak compound in the Mojave Desert called Boron. From the air it appears even more desolate and lonely than along the empty two-lane highway far below.

Many people who know Tei Fu's story are still uncomfortable at the mention of Boron, preferring that these difficult issues of fairness and justice be sealed tightly in a box and placed on a shelf. A handful of others portray Boron as the ultimate symbol of failure, and mail anonymous packages to the news media.

To me, Boron stands as a symbol of triumph—as the reflection of the iron will of a man and woman named Chen, and the people who call themselves Sunriders. The top of any mountain appears most majestically, not when observed from above but when viewed from the deep valley floor below. With the Chens and their Sunrider distributors,

I have seen both the peaks and the valleys, and watched the struggles of the journey through both.

My journey is better because of theirs. The highest peaks, for all of us, rise somewhere still ahead. Invariably, our paths will lead us there. Someplace where the sun is rising. Someplace where the shadows are behind.

SOURCES

This book is based largely on primary sources, including the author's own professional involvement with Drs. Tei Fu and Oi-Lin Chen, and Sunrider, over the past decade. The Chens have been gracious and generous with their time, submitting to candid interviews to fill in the gaps, particularly during their growing-up years in their Asian homelands and the early period after they immigrated to the United States and established Sunrider.

Other sources include the writings of or interviews with principals named in the book, notably a number of Sunrider distributors, attorneys, and others with first-hand knowledge of the birth and growth of Sunrider International. Transcripts of key meetings, newspaper and periodical articles, and various legal documents–a number of which are cited below–also helped ensure the accuracy of *Journey to the Sun*.

Chapter Two   Tradition

Page 14   The standard reference on Confucius is *The Analects of Confucius*, one of the most influential books in Chinese history. It was edited by a congress of Confucius' disciples shortly after his death in 479 B.C. A number of English-language editions are available, including one translated by Simon Leys, W.W. Norton & Company, 1997.

Chapter Four   Wisdom of the Ancients

Page 32   The name Sheng Nung can be translated as Divine Farmer. One of the greatest heroes of Chinese culture, he taught the people how to farm as well as how to use herbs. See one of the three foundation books of Chinese medicine; Yang Shou-Zhong, translator, *The Divine Farmer's Materia Medica* (Boulder, Colorado: Blue Poppy Press, 1999).

Page 34   Hippocrates was a very influential Greek physician of about the fifth century B.C. His writings had a lasting impact on the practice and ethics of medicine. Those about to begin medical practice today still take the Hippocratic oath embodying his code of conduct.

Page 35   The Yellow Emperor is regarded, along with Sheng Nung, as one of the icons of Chinese culture. See Maoshing Ni, translator, *The Yellow Emperor's Classic of Medicine: A New Translation of the Neijing Suwen With Commentary* (Boston, Shambhala Publications, 1995).

Chapter Five   Yin and Yang

Page 42   . . . *he applied to Kaoshiung Medical College and was accepted.;* Kaoshiung is the only medical college in the lower half of Taiwan. About 100,000 students graduated from high school in Taiwan at the same time as Tei Fu; approximately 1,000 of them were admitted to medical school in Taiwan, including 400 who went to Kaoshiung.

Page 46   *He excelled at judo as well as other Chinese martial arts.;* Tei Fu won first or second place in a number of national judo competitions in Taiwan. Later, in the U.S., he again placed first or second in Rocky Mountain regional contests. Tei Fu holds black belts in judo, karate, and aikido.

Chapter Six   Two Become One

Page 57   *The reference to Tei Fu as "Dr. Chen" was entirely proper in Taiwan . . . ;* Even in the West the title is not entirely inappropriate. Definitions of "doctor" in a standard Webster's dictionary include "a learned or authoritative teacher," "a person awarded an honorary doctorate" [Tei Fu Chen was awarded such a doctorate from China Cultural University, Taiwan, in 1990], or "one skilled or specializing in the healing arts." *Webster's Ninth New Collegiate Dictionary* (Springfield, Mass., Merriam-Webster Inc., 1989), 371.

Chapter Eight   Dreams of Parents

Page 79   Nature's Sunshine and Nature's Way, pioneers in introducing herbal nutrition commercially to the United States about three decades ago, were both still in business and headquartered in Utah County as of 1999.

Chapter Nine   East Meets West

Page 95   Ken Murdock, president and CEO of Nature's Way, was the son of Tom Murdock, who founded the company in 1968 after finding that a desert herb growing near the family home in Arizona greatly improved the health of his critically ill wife.

Chapter Ten   Walk With Destiny

Page 107 *After only one month in business, Sunrider published* . . . ; The first *SunWriter* was dated January 1983. While explaining the health benefits of herbal foods, the company's official publication from the start emphasized that "Sunrider does not prescribe the use of herbs as a form of treatment for any ailment without medical approval." Succeeding issues of *SunWriter* continued to carry the same statement.

Page 108   . . . *the importance of creating a motivating marketing and compensation plan* . . . ; Black spelled out the plan in great detail in the June 1983 *SunWriter,* saying it met three critical goals: "First, we give our distributors the highest possible earnings. Second, we keep the price of our products fair. And third, we protect the financial stability of the company."

Page 110 *In July 1983 Chen introduced his Auto Fund program.* (in *SunWriter*); Distributors reaching the Group Director level were eligible to buy the vehicles of their choice and earn the full value of the cars and all costs of ownership over the next 24 months by their personal sales volume and that of their downline directors.

Page 111 *"As construction progressed, it became evident that one individual . . . "*; October/November 1983 *SunWriter*.

Chapter Eleven   Clouds on the Horizon

Page 118 *"Sunriders, we are facing a challenge."*; Statement of Tei Fu Chen to convention participants. A close variation of his statement appeared in written form in the July 1984 *SunWriter*.

Chapter Twelve   California Sun

Page 136 . . . *Tei Fu felt impressed that the company should move its headquarters to Southern California*; In the 1987 Issue No. 1 of *Sun-Writer*, he explained: "I'm so excited! . . . So many good things have happened and are going to happen in the near future that I can hardly contain myself . . . Over the last several months we have purchased a new facility in Torrance, California, . . . and reached an all-time high monthly sales mark."

Chapter Thirteen   Sharks in the Water

Page 145 *A reporter named Con Psarras targeted Sunrider . . .*; Psarras was KSL's lone full-time investigative reporter, and as such was given unusual latitude in preparing his stories, which were often featured during ratings months.

Page 150 *College student Teena Horlacher summarized her report on KSL . . .*; Horlacher ended her 21-page study by asking of KSL, the longtime news leader in its market, "How can a professional TV news station . . . air this report? A report which has no basis of truth, but hype. Where is the accountability?"

Page 151 *"A recent Herald article incorrectly . . . "*; The letter to the editor by Paul Jensen appeared in the Provo *Herald*. Jensen sent an almost identical letter to the *Salt Lake Tribune*, the state's largest newspaper, which ran it on March 15, 1991.

Page 152 . . . *Debi Boling filed a lawsuit, . . .*; *Debi A. Boling vs. The Sunrider Corporation and Tei Fu Chen*, U.S. District Court, District of Arizona, February 1988. The trial itself began on December 17, 1991.

Chapter Fourteen   A House Divided

Page 159 *Records show that the check likely ended up in an account* . . . ; Much of the money was still there as of June 2, 1989, when Central Bank's head teller Gaye Lynn Jacobson issued a notice "To Whom It May Concern" saying "Jau-Fei Chen has a balance in this bank of $923,965.77."

Page 164 . . . *attorney Stephen Hard acknowledged what Tei Fu had long suspected* . . . ; Letter from Hard to Judge Greene, dated December 7, 1992.

Chapter Fifteen   Piercing the Heart

Page 169 *Everything that E. Excel did in the early years* . . . ; An undated brochure entitled "Meet E. Excel!" laid out the company's herbal philosophy, parroting, without attribution, the writings of Sunrider's Tei Fu Chen that began appearing years earlier in the *SunWriter* newsletter.

Page 170 *She openly admitted her lack of herbal knowledge* . . . ; Jau-Fei Chen's interview ran in the Provo *Herald* on April 30, 1989.

Page 181 *One magazine story ran the headline "American Food 'Sunrider' Kills People."*; The false story, published December 9, 1990 in *Ta Ming Pao*, a Taiwanese periodical, named Tei Fu's father as the source for information "that in Taiwan, two or three deaths of consumers have already occurred as a result of taking [Sunrider] products."

Chapter Sixteen   Rising to the Challenge

Page 193 *Ignoring the evidence* . . . *the jury returned a guilty verdict* . . . ; The verdict was rendered on March 30, 1992.

Chapter Seventeen   Full Circle

Page 197 *Andrews wanted to come clean.*; His startling voluntary confession to the attorneys in Arizona covered two days, May 26 and 27, 1993. The highly detailed interviews with Andrews were tape-recorded, with his knowledge, filling a written transcript of more than 140 pages.

Page 202 *"I heard about Mickey Cochran from Con Psarras . . ."*;
If true, Psarras had flaunted journalistic ethics by becoming an advocate
against Sunrider and privately aiding its enemies. The Society of Professional Journalists–America's largest such organization–states that "Journalists should be free of obligation to any interest other than the
public's right to know," and warns them to "remain free of associations
and activities that may compromise integrity or damage credibility." SPJ
Code of Ethics, adopted in 1926 and last revised in 1996.

Chapter Nineteen   Climb to the Top

Page 234 . . . *"we've caught the big koi fish now."*; koi fish are
prized in Asian cultures.

Page 236 . . . *upon leaving Sunrider Jau-Hwa had taken with her
. . .* ; In four days of depositions–July 9, 1991, March 6, 1992, and
March 20-21, 1992–Jau-Hwa admitted spiriting away from Sunrider a
stack of documents she measured for interrogators by holding her
hands inches apart. *Sunrider Corp. vs. E. Excel International*, United
States District Court for Utah.

Chapter Twenty   Dawn of a New Decade

Page 244 . . . *the official opening of the spectacular $35 million
facility . . . ;* Included in Sunrider's three-story World Headquarters are
high-tech offices, a 500-seat Grand Ballroom, a luxurious cafeteria, VIP
lounge, multi-purpose theater, and full-scale gallery. A 50,000-square-
foot expansion was being added in the summer of 1999.

Page 249 . . . *Moyers explained that he went to China . . .* ; Moyers
also wrote that "Although traditional Chinese medicine feels alien to
Westerners like me . . . I can see that it may have something to offer . . ."
Echoing what Tei Fu Chen had long taught, Moyers added that "health
is not just an absence of illness, it is a way of living." (New York: Double-
day, 1993), 308.

Chapter Twenty-One   Triumph and Tragedy

Page 260 . . . *"Jau-Fei performed more than ten years of cancer
research" . . . ;* "E. Excel International: A Profile of Excellence," 1997, 5.

Page 260 . . . *"Nutritional Immunology," a science which she claims to have "created,"*; Ibid.

Page 260 . . . *"I'll at least guarantee you one hundred and ten years old . . . "*; Transcript of Jau-Fei Chen's lecture at an E. Excel seminar in the Philippines, November 1998, 31.

Chapter Twenty-Three   Failed Justice

Page 281 . . . *The Chen sisters succeeded . . .* ; Letter from Vincent J. Marella to Michael J. Dempsey, U.S. Justice Department, Los Angeles, California, October 27, 1997.

Page 282 *Caplin wrote: "The government's case against Mr. Chen . . . "*; Letter from Mortimer Caplin to U.S. Department of Justice, October 28, 1997.

Page 288 *" . . . the prosecutor's job isn't just to win, but to win fairly, . . . "*; Judge Alex Kozinski, *United States vs. Kojayan*, U.S. Ninth Circuit Court of Appeals, 1993. Five years after Judge Kozinski's warning, prosecutorial misconduct was still a serious problem. A two-year investigation by the Pittsburgh *Post-Gazette* found "examples of prosecutors lying, hiding evidence, distorting the facts, engaging in cover-ups, paying for perjury and setting up innocent people to win indictments, guilty pleas and convictions." Associated Press story in *The Salt Lake Tribune*, November 22, 1998.

Page 289 *In late 1996, Olsen filed a thirty-three page motion, . . . ;* The motion to dismiss the indictment because of government misconduct was filed in United States District Court, Central District of California, Southern Division, November 18, 1996.

Epilogue

Page 307 *"[We] travel sometimes dangerously, sometimes safely . . ."*; Spencer W. Kimball, *The Miracle of Forgiveness* (Salt Lake City, Utah, Bookcraft, 1969), 1.